Fighting Global Warming:

A Problematic Economic Integration

Problematic Economic Implications

References for the data:

References for the data can be cross-checked by searching the Internet for the keywords in the text. Otherwise, the author can be contacted through the website findtheflaw.com.

Acknowledgments:

Editing and feedback about text accessibility: Margaret Strubel.

Fighting Global Warming: Problematic Economic Implications

(+ A parallel market to bypass political deadlock)

Vincent Lannoye

In memory of my mother.

TABLE OF CONTENTS

Alphabetical Index

Introduction

3. Governments Nudging Timidly the Economy

ALPHABETICAL INDEX

INTRODUCTION

Paying for climate action and reaching net-zero emissions ultimately comes down to money—but it is not as simple as it sounds. Transitioning from fossil fuels to clean energy requires major investment, and governments face a difficult task: securing the necessary funds without undermining employment.

Too many place blind faith in higher taxes and stricter regulations as easy fixes, but this belief often stems from misunderstandings about how money actually works—making climate debates more polarized than necessary. In reality, modern money is no longer like the gold coins of the past, when wealth was tied to precious metals. Today, money is simply a unit of account, not real wealth stored in a vault. The idea that governments can simply seize banknotes to solve any problem is an illusion. This book calls it the "money delusion." Understanding how money truly works is essential for having realistic conversations about climate action.

Not fooled by this delusion, most economists oppose broad tax hikes to fund climate action. They are not calling for governments to take money by force from individuals or businesses. Instead, their usual recommendation is modest carbon taxes that nudge consumers away from fossil fuels while staying within the existing market system. The aim is to influence energy use, not to have governments fully finance the green transition.

That said, these same economists have yet to figure out how to make clean energy more profitable than fossil fuels while ensuring adequate job creation. In fact, their track record in handling major crises is mixed. From the Great Depression of the 1930s to the energy shocks of the 1970s—and now the green transition—economists have often struggled to provide effective solutions, as discussed in *The History of Money for Understanding Economics* (see final page).

This doesn't mean market-based solutions without new taxes are impossible—there may be other approaches worth exploring.

Part 1

GLOBAL WARMING

IS HAPPENING

The fight against climate change is at a standstill. Climate skeptics often fail to recognize that the threat is urgent—or even real. Former Senator Jim Inhofe famously mocked global warming by holding up a snowball in Congress. Such skeptics question not only the scientific consensus but also the astronomical cost of any meaningful green transition.

Criticism, however, should not spare green advocates who ignore economic realities. A transition cannot push people into poverty or hardship while privileged elites remain largely unaffected. Real solutions must benefit everyone—not just a select few—or the majority will push back against unfair policies. Progress may only come through creative and unconventional thinking.

Before diving into economic considerations in later pages, it is important to understand the basic principles behind global warming. At its core, this is a problem rooted in physics and technology.

Unabated Climate Change

Failure to contain climate change

Scientists have been sounding the alarm for decades about the acceleration of *"global warming,"* also known as *"climate change."* This phenomenon is driven by the release of carbon dioxide (*"CO_2"*), methane (CH_4), nitrous oxide (N_2O), and other less common gases into the atmosphere—primarily from the widespread burning of fossil fuels to power industrial processes. These gases, together with naturally occurring water vapor, intensify the *"greenhouse effect"* by trapping solar radiation and warming the atmosphere. For this reason, they are collectively known as *"greenhouse gases"* (*"GHGs"*).

Despite these scientific warnings, global temperatures continue to rise with little intervention, as emissions have increased steadily since the Industrial Revolution. Since the ratification of the Kyoto Protocol in 1997 by 192 nations—and through subsequent Conferences of the Parties (COPs)—global efforts to reduce GHG emissions have remained insufficient. Nations have made only limited commitments, and as a result, concerns are escalating while the global economy continues to spew emissions.

Many demonstrations are calling for stronger regulations to combat global warming. However, there is no silver bullet. Financial resources are limited, and misconceptions about available funding abound. Regulations must be effective without becoming overly authoritarian or placing disproportionate burdens on low-income communities. Instead, they should offer clear, shared benefits. So far, no government has managed to achieve this balance. Addressing climate change cannot come at the cost of deepening inequality —but should it be accepted that there is no alternative path forward?

Falling behind on COP21's 2030 targets

As of 2024, the greenhouse gas reduction targets set under the COP21 Paris Agreement appear increasingly out of reach, as global emissions continue to rise. Meeting these goals would require a 45% reduction in global emissions by 2030 and achieving net zero by 2050.

• United States:
The US has decreased its GHG emissions by about 18% from their peak in 2005 to 2023. This reduction is primarily due to the transition from coal-fired power plants to more economical natural gas power plants, as natural gas combustion releases approximately 50% less CO_2 than coal for an equivalent amount of energy produced.

Despite this progress, the US is not on track to achieve its emissions reduction goals. The original commitment aimed to reduce overall GHG emissions by 26 to 28 percent below 2005 levels by 2025. In 2024, the unmet target was revised to a more ambitious goal of reducing emissions by 61 to 66 percent by 2035.

• European Union:
The EU achieved a reduction in emissions by about 30% between 1990 and 2023. This decline can be attributed to factors such as milder winters, economic downturns around 2001, 2008 and 2020, improvements in energy efficiency, the substitution of coal with natural gas imported from Russia and Norway, and the development of new renewable energy facilities.

Currently, the EU is not on track to achieve its target of reducing emissions by "at least 55%" by 2030.

• For the World:
Globally, GHG emissions have risen by approximately 24% between 2005 and 2024. The primary culprit is coal-fired power generation, which continues to grow in countries such as Turkey, Indonesia, China, India and Russia. These nations have not yet reached peak coal, although the rate of emission growth has slowed over the past decade. This trend could drive atmospheric carbon dioxide levels above 800 parts per million—levels not seen on Earth for nearly 50 million years.

Approaching 2°C by 2050: Entering the danger zone

Between 2014 to 2023, the Earth's average surface temperature rose by a record 1.2°C since the onset of the Industrial Revolution in the 19th century, with annual variations influenced by the ocean's absorption of heat.

The coming decades are expected to be even warmer. Advanced climate models, driven by state-of-the-art supercomputing, predict that global temperatures could rise at a rate currently estimated at 0.20°C per decade—even if all nations meet their greenhouse gas reduction commitments under the COP21 Paris Agreement. Alarmingly, the rate of warming appears to be accelerating, potentially reaching 0.25°C or possibly 0.30°C per decade.

At this pace, total warming could reach around 2°C by 2050, surpassing the 1.5°C threshold that scientists consider critical for avoiding severe climate impacts. The UN's net-zero target by 2050 was designed to keep global temperatures below 1.5°C—or at the very least, under 2°C. Urgent progress is needed to stay within these limits.

The greenhouse effect feeds on solar radiation and on infrared radiation re-emitted by the Earth's surface, which is heated by the Sun.

Fortunately, this infrared radiation or "heat radiation"—at the core of the greenhouse effect—has kept Earth's surface temperatures warm during the night for millions of years.

Unfortunately, however, a slight imbalance of greenhouse gases linked to human activity is increasing the trapping of infrared radiation, causing average temperatures to rise. This phenomenon, known as global warming or climate change, has been gradually overheating the planet since the onset of the Industrial Revolution.

In detail, solar radiation heats up the Earth in different ways:
• Incoming (visible) sunlight travels through the transparent atmosphere, heating black objects that absorb sunlight, as well as colored objects or liquids (e.g., seawater) that absorb sunlight while reflecting some light, which appears as colors to the human eye.
• Incoming infrared radiation from the Sun is mostly reflected (i.e., absorbed and re-emitted in all directions) back to space by the atmosphere, which is "not-so-transparent" to infrared radiation. In other words, solar infrared radiation is partially absorbed by the gases in the atmosphere, heating them, while some radiation manages to reach the Earth's surface and to heat it. These "non-transparent" atmospheric gases are the so-called greenhouse gases, such as—in order of importance—water vapor, carbon dioxide, methane, and nitrous oxide. Nitrogen and oxygen, on the other hand, are transparent to infrared radiation.
• Outgoing infrared radiation is re-emitted by the Earth's surface and the atmosphere warmed by solar radiation. This outgoing infrared radiation bounces (i.e., absorbed and re-emitted) as "heat radiation"—either escaping into space, being trapped in the atmosphere, or, to some extent, radiating back toward the Earth's surface.
• Incoming solar ultraviolet radiation plays a very small role in heating the Earth's surface, as most of it is absorbed by the ozone layer in the upper atmosphere.

Vulnerable nations could become unlivable by 2100

Failure to curb carbon emissions could raise global temperatures by up to 4°C by 2100. This level of unchecked warming—driven by an intensifying greenhouse effect—could severely destabilize the Earth's climate and oceans. Large regions may become unlivable due to extreme heat or flooding, forcing mass migration toward cooler and more stable areas.

Countries in the tropics are expected to be the hardest hit, as their already hot climates and geographic location make them particularly vulnerable. Compounding this challenge is their limited capacity to adapt to rising temperatures, as many of these nations are among the poorest in the world.

• Arid regions, including the Sahel and the Mediterranean, could experience persistent droughts, increasing the risks of fires, depleting fresh water and food supply, as their arable land or grazing fields transform into desert.

• These countries may endure lethal heatwaves accompanied by high humidity, which prevents the human body from cooling through perspiration. They could face up to 200 days per year of extreme heat risks, with occasional heatwaves that could destroy crops, harm livestock, or even cause heat-related deaths, particularly among the elderly.

Coastal populations, including many cities worldwide, may be on the front lines of global warming in the coming decades:

• Melting Arctic ice may raise sea levels and submerge coastal land, forcing populations to relocate.

• Hurricanes may grow stronger, causing more devastating impacts on coastlines.

• Fishermen may face the collapse of fish stocks as ocean acidification from CO_2 absorption disrupts marine life.

Adaptation efforts by the most affected populations may prove too costly and too slow, forcing them to migrate in search of dry land, clean water, or food. Such pressures could escalate into border clashes or even guerrilla warfare.

Passing the peak of CO_2 emissions won't stop their accumulation

GHG emissions, and particularly CO_2, must do more than merely peak and stop increasing; the current rate of emissions is too high. This concentration of CO_2 in the atmosphere has increased from 280 ppm —parts-per-million—in the pre-industrial era to above 400 ppm after

2016. At this rate, CO_2 continues to accumulate in the atmosphere, necessitating a drastic reduction in emissions to absolute zero.

A concentration of 400 ppm of carbon dioxide (CO_2) is well above what the Earth's natural systems can absorb. Oceans, forests, soil, and other carbon sinks remove some CO_2 from the atmosphere, but not enough to offset current levels. Vegetation on land and in the oceans absorbs CO_2 through photosynthesis, converting it into oxygen and organic matter.

Rain also removes a small amount of CO_2 from the air as it falls—a process known as "wet deposition," where CO_2 dissolves in water. However, this has only a minor effect on reducing overall atmospheric CO_2. Much of the CO_2 absorbed by rainwater eventually ends up in the oceans, where it may later be released back into the atmosphere.

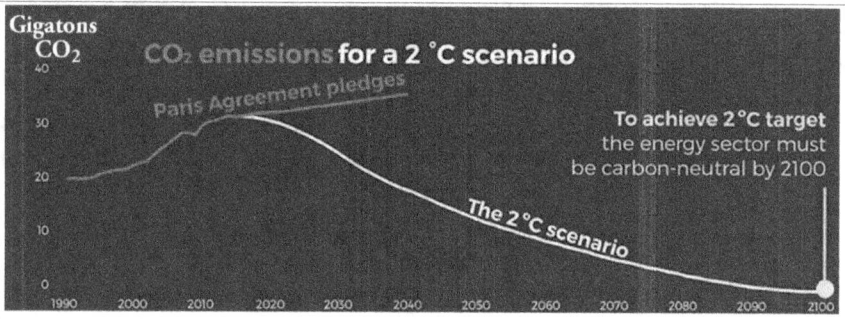

The area under the curve represents the maximum amount of "emissions stored in the atmosphere" needed to stay below a 2-degree Celsius increase.

In red, the trend of CO_2 emissions, as visible in the 2013 "World Energy Outlook" by the IEA, shows no signs of declining, even with the reduction targets set by the Paris Agreement of COP21.

In white, the curve indicates the necessary trajectory for emissions to reach zero by 2100 in order to stay below the 2-degree Celsius threshold, considering past, current, and future emissions accumulating in the atmosphere.

Net zero as soon as possible—delays make recovery harder

GHG emissions must rapidly reach net zero by 2050 to halt further temperature increases, which would otherwise threaten coastal communities through rising sea levels, intensifies heatwaves, and disrupts ecosystems. CO_2 emissions also contribute to ocean acidification, posing serious risks to marine life.

A prompt decline in CO_2 emissions is particularly important to mitigate the long-term risks associated with the accumulation of CO_2 at high altitudes, where it is less likely to be absorbed by oceans or vegetation. Unlike CO_2 at lower altitudes, high-altitude CO_2 poses challenges for natural absorption processes—or even through man-made carbon capture technologies.

Beyond net zero: The case for net negative

Any delay in reaching net-zero emissions may force the world to go further, requiring net-negative carbon strategies—actively removing CO_2 from the atmosphere. These efforts, known as Carbon Dioxide Removal (CDR) technologies, are already included in the UN's Intergovernmental Panel on Climate Change (IPCC) scenarios for limiting global warming to below 1.5°C, or for reducing atmospheric CO_2 concentrations to levels that could eventually bring temperatures back below that threshold.

In fact, net-negative targets may need to go even further to stabilize melting glaciers and ice sheets. Future efforts might aim to lower global temperatures well below the 1.5°C threshold. Research shows that even at the 1.2°C average warming recorded around 2020, both Greenland and Antarctica experienced significant ice loss. Many scientists believe a global average closer to 1°C may be necessary to ensure long-term ice sheet stability.

Carbon removal can be achieved through a combination of technological and nature-based methods. Technological approaches include systems that capture CO_2 from the air—similar to the air-scrubbing systems used in submarines—with the captured carbon stored underground. Nature-based solutions involve reforestation, improved farming practices, and land management techniques that enhance the carbon content of soil. Experimental concepts also include high-altitude balloons equipped with capture systems to remove CO_2 lingering at higher elevations.

This net-negative approach focuses specifically on carbon dioxide. Other greenhouse gases—such as methane—must still be reduced, but they are naturally removed from the atmosphere through oxidation over a relatively short timescale of 7 to 12 years.

Reducing GHG Emissions to Prevent Severe Warming

Economic output and GHG emissions

Human activities are identified as primary contributors to the rising concentration of carbon dioxide, methane, and nitrous oxide in the Earth's atmosphere. These increases are mostly attributed to three sectors:

The energy sector is responsible for emitting about 75% of global GHG emissions:

• Energy comes predominantly from the burning of *"fossil fuels,"* comprising coal, natural gas, and petroleum derivatives like gasoline. These energy sources, when combusted in the presence of oxygen (O_2), release carbon dioxide (*"CO_2"*) into the atmosphere as a byproduct. Additionally, the extraction processes for these fuels result in the release of methane (CH_4) into the atmosphere.

Agriculture and deforestation make up most of the remaining 25% of global GHG emissions:

• Agriculture is generating methane and nitrous oxide from organic waste decomposition, from livestock farming, or from the use of fertilizers. These gases are potent contributors to the greenhouse effect aside from CO_2 emissions.

• Deforestation not only prevents the absorption of CO_2 by trees, but also releases CO_2 and methane from decomposing vegetation.

The consumption of fossil fuels does not have its roots in capitalism. As detailed in the book referenced on the last page, capitalism emerged in the 16th century, two centuries before extensive coal mining began. Its primary purpose was to finance trading ventures, such as those undertaken by the wind-powered ships of the Dutch East India Company.

Later, capitalism funded early industrialization in the 18th century, which did not initially rely on coal to power machinery. The first factories of the Industrial Revolution, such as those in Great Britain, were powered by large waterwheels. In the United States, the first textile mills such as the Slater Mill in the picture, built in the 1790s, also utilized water power.

It was only in the 19th century that steam engines powered by coal began to replace hydraulic power extensively. Coal's consistent availability, unlike the seasonal variability of water power, and the ability to locate factories away from rivers made coal a preferred energy source. This British model of coal-based industrialization was adopted worldwide, regardless of whether the industrialization process followed a capitalist framework, as in the Western world, or a communist model, as in the USSR in the 20th century.

Instead of coal, electrical technologies, such as the arc furnace for steel in 1810, the electric motor in 1824, and the dynamo in 1832 could have complemented hydro-power during the 19th century. Electricity could have been generated by waterwheels, windmills and electric batteries to power electric motors. Without fossil fuels, the Industrial Revolution might have progressed more slowly but could have happened anyway.

Shares of GHG emissions by economic sector

Human-induced GHG emissions originate from corporations, farms and households. Emissions of carbon dioxide, methane, nitrous oxide, and other gases can be classified by economic sector and compared after converting them into a common unit of CO_2 equivalents. Each gas is converted based on its capacity to trap heat in the atmosphere. This conversion enables comparison across sectors and is used to calculate each sector's *"carbon footprint"* in CO_2 equivalents.

Source	Short description	Emissions percentage for US / World (figures: 2017 eia.gov)
Electric power plants	Coal and natural gas for turbines.	US:28% / World:25%
Industry	Oil and coal industry's own emissions (for its own exploitation and distribution), and other industries' natural gas for ovens, coal for steel mills, and other industrial processes.	US:22% / World:31%
Transports	Gas and diesel for engines in cars, trucks, airplanes, boats, railroads...	US:29% / World:14%
Residential and commercial	Heating oil for furnaces, natural gas for stoves, methane from waste decomposition...	US:12% / World:6%
Agriculture	Methane from waste decomposition, CO_2 from tilling, etc....	US:9% / World:24%
Negative Source	Short description	Mitigates previous figures
CO_2 removed by ecosystems	Forests can absorb CO_2, but they shouldn't excuse countries with large ecosystems (e.g., Amazon rainforest) from going carbon-free.	Reforestation/deforestation is measured with satellites such as NASA's Landsat or GEDI from ISS

Altogether, the burning of fossil fuels accounts for about 75% of global GHG emissions, while the rest comes mostly from agriculture and deforestation minus natural absorption by ecosystems.

Main culprit: Fossil fuels as an energy source

Energy becomes a crucial aspect of global warming, as 80% of global energy generation comes from fossil fuels. This figure comes from the IEA (International Energy Agency), which strives to gather data from individual countries. For instance, the US provides data through its EIA (Energy Information Administration).

Only the remaining 20% of global energy is not based on fossil fuels. This last energy category encompasses different energy sources such as nuclear, hydroelectric, geothermal, solar and wind.

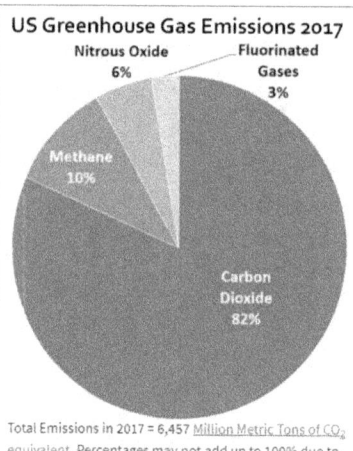

US Greenhouse Gas Emissions 2017

Nitrous Oxide 6%
Fluorinated Gases 3%
Methane 10%
Carbon Dioxide 82%

Total Emissions in 2017 = 6,457 Million Metric Tons of CO₂ equivalent. Percentages may not add up to 100% due to independent rounding.

Energy from cheap fossil fuels is the principal culprit of global warming. First, the combustion of fossil fuels generates most CO2 emissions. Second, the extraction of fossil fuels releases methane emissions due to careless leaking from extraction and refining of coal and gas.

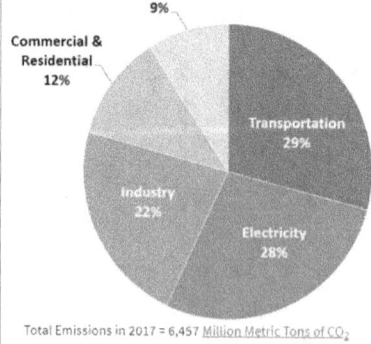

Total US Greenhouse Gas Emissions by Economic Sector in 2017

Agriculture 9%
Commercial & Residential 12%
Transportation 29%
Industry 22%
Electricity 28%

Total Emissions in 2017 = 6,457 Million Metric Tons of CO₂ equivalent. Percentages may not add up to 100% due to independent rounding.

Individuals cannot solely attribute responsibility to corporations as the primary source of CO2 emissions from burning fossil fuels. People indirectly consume fossil fuels through electricity generated by dirty power plants, cheap products manufactured by corporations that run on fossil fuels, and food from intensive agriculture, all of which are transported by gasoline-powered vehicles.

Electricity is only a fraction of global energy use

According to the IEA, electricity generation consumes approximately 20% of global energy, with two-thirds of electricity derived from fossil fuels and one-third from other energy sources. In the US, the EIA reports that electricity accounts for about 17% of national energy consumption, with two-thirds of it also coming from fossil fuels.

Based on this figure, overhauling power plants to renewable energy sources will not suffice to curb global warming, given that electricity generation represents only a portion of global energy consumption.

When perusing news articles regarding green energy data, it is important to distinguish whether the figures pertain to energy as a whole or specifically to electricity, as journalists often conflate the two terms. For example, a report on the United States achieving a record-breaking 40% share of zero-carbon electricity in 2022 can be misleading. In reality, this 40% only translates to clean energy accounting for 6.8% of total energy consumption (6.8% = 40% of 17%, as electricity represents 17% of the total energy mix in the US). This 6.8% falls short of being a notable milestone in the battle against climate change.

Western Nations Must Lead the Way

Emission cuts in the West but increases in the Global South

Global GHG emissions continue to rise relentlessly. Efforts by Western nations to cut their emissions have fallen short, achieving only modest reductions that fail to offset the much larger increases from emerging economies in the Global South.

Meanwhile, industrialization in the Global South has surged. Countries such as China, India, Brazil, and Indonesia have followed the Western model of development, heavily relying on coal and petroleum to fuel their growing economies since the late 20th century.

This trend risks accelerating global warming, potentially pushing the temperature rise to 0.30°C per decade, with the hottest years reaching a 4°C increase by 2100.

The sluggishness of industrialized nations despite historic responsibility

Given their past CO_2 emissions, the wealthiest nations are expected to lead by example and drastically reduce their GHG emissions before the rest of the world. However, they have not met these expectations. Rich industrial nations have responded poorly to the challenge of global warming, despite their historically high per-capita emissions since the Industrial Revolution in the 19th century.

Is Trump solely to blame for unstoppable global warming following the US withdrawal from the Paris agreements (COP21)? Not entirely.

Both Democrats and Republicans fall short in addressing the broader challenges of climate change, as it will be discussed in the following sections.

In short, the Democratic Party has yet to propose an effective regulatory alternative to accelerate the green transition. So far, it has opposed certain measures that could be important for achieving a net-zero future—such as expanding nuclear energy, approving mining permits, and easing regulations, even for environmentally focused companies. It cannot reasonably ask the public to act while tying their hands behind their backs. Nor can it place blame on low-income individuals who resist high green costs or fear job losses in industries such as coal mining.

Meanwhile, Trump promoted research in safer nuclear power and his tax cuts may have provided some support for green technology. Perhaps, Republicans may have prioritized natural gas and petroleum from fracking, but so have Democrats. Both parties acknowledge several economic benefits of this approach: it replaces coal, which has higher GHG emissions; creates domestic jobs; reduces dependence on petroleum imports; narrows the US foreign trade deficit; and strengthens the country's long-term position in international financial markets.

Outsourcing industrial GHG emissions to the Global South

Wealthy nations have not only exported a polluting industrial model to the Global South but have also outsourced part of their own GHG emissions, particularly since the globalization boom of the post–Cold War era. Countries such as China, India, and Vietnam produce goods for the Western world at lower costs while generating substantial emissions—especially in energy-intensive sectors like steel, cement, and heavy manufacturing destined for export to wealthier nations.

This practice raises important questions about how GHG emissions are accounted for. A reassessment is needed to determine whether consumers, rather than solely producers, should be held accountable for the emissions associated with the goods they import. It also casts further doubt on the already modest emission-reduction figures reported by wealthy nations.

Recent efforts by these same rich nations to re-industrialize, driven by geopolitical tensions, may help clarify the true GHG footprint of domestic consumption, as manufacturing processes are shifted back into domestic supply chains.

Political and geopolitical risks of climate leadership

Wealthy nations face significant challenges in demonstrating credible leadership in the global fight against climate change. Providing a viable model for clean and affordable energy alternatives to developing countries is crucial. However, progress remains insufficient. The lack of technological advancements that make clean energy economically accessible to both industrialized nations and the Global South continues to impede meaningful progress.

Compounding this issue is the persistent lack of trust stemming from unfulfilled promises of financial support. The stalled progress in negotiations at the UN Conferences of the Parties (COP) has further hindered decisive climate action in developing nations. The inability of wealthier countries to honor commitments to compensate poorer nations for climate-related impacts has eroded trust, weakened cooperation, and exacerbated the delays in implementing global solutions.

Addressing these risks requires stronger leadership, tangible results from technological investments, and a renewed commitment to equitable climate solutions that bridge the gap between the Western world and the Global South.

Failure by wealthy nations to innovate and deliver affordable clean energy alternatives to fossil fuels could have dangerous consequences, including:

• Political Polarization in Wealthy Nations: The inability to address climate change contributes to disillusionment and resurrects radical communist ideologies, particularly among younger generations.

• Increased Fossil Fuel Consumption in Developing Countries: Developing nations, prioritizing economic growth, may accelerate their reliance on coal and petroleum while holding wealthy nations accountable for failing to provide clean energy alternatives.

• Rising Migration: Worsening climate conditions in the Global South may drive migration to the milder climates of the Western world, further straining already polarized politics.

• Emergence of a Global South Alliance: A coalition of nations in the Global South, disproportionately impacted by global warming, could form in opposition to the perceived inaction of wealthy nations.

China and its president, Xi Jinping, remain steadfast in their belief that "capitalism is bound to die out and socialism is bound to win." Guided by this vision, China's meteoric growth is evident in its advancements in solar panels and batteries—technologies developed not only to combat severe domestic air pollution, which has plagued cities like Beijing, but also to expand its influence among nations grappling with the impacts of global warming.

China's initial attempt to expand its global influence through the Belt and Road Initiative faced setbacks due to overreach and heavy-handed tactics. However, it may have a second chance if the United States neglects green priorities, risking alienation from its allies and ultimately allowing its influence to dwindle to the benefit of China and its authoritarian regime.

Part 2

NO EASY SOLUTION FOR

GOVERNMENTS

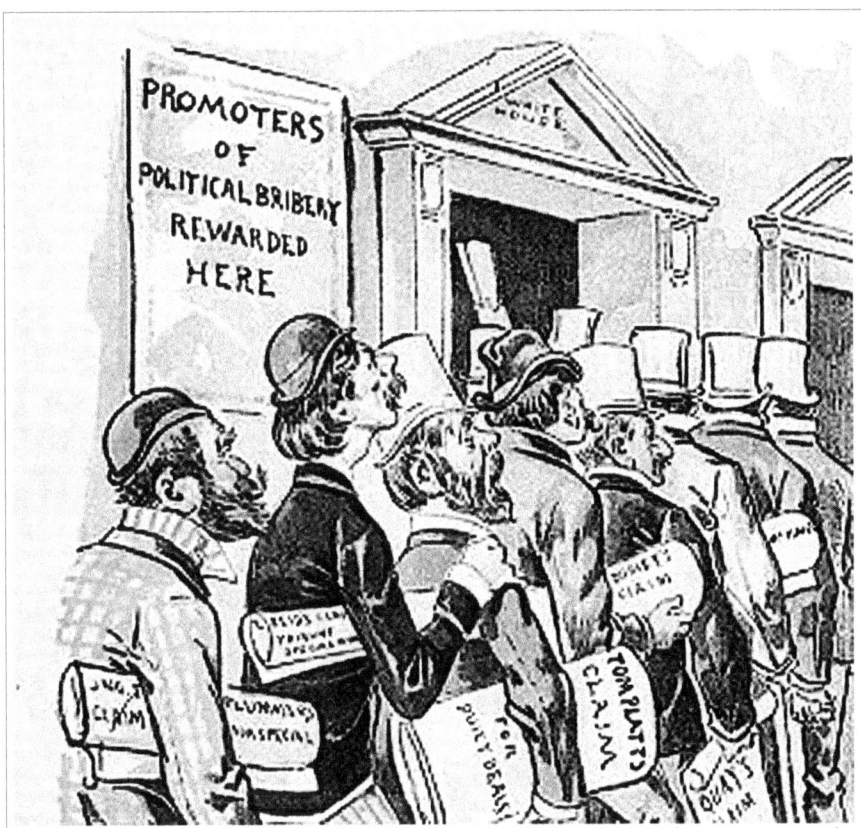

Are wealthy lobbyists bribing politicians to avoid action on climate change? Not exactly. The issue is more complex, as the next section will explain. Governments struggle because economists haven't found a reliable way to raise funds to fight climate change without risking job losses. Many doubt that government policies alone can fix the issue without also causing unemployment. Instead, they often suggest leaving most of the work to market forces.

No, Clean Energy Cannot Simply Be Made Mandatory

Mandatory clean energy?

Clean energy sources—such as solar, wind, and even nuclear—offer viable alternatives to fossil fuels for electricity generation, as technological advancements continue to improve the efficiency of capturing solar and wind energy and as newer nuclear plants become safer. This would be even more the case if the production of solar panels, wind turbines, and standardized small modular nuclear reactors could increase to mass-production levels, thereby reducing per-unit costs.

Given these advantages, it seems time to mandate that power plants, corporations, and households transition to clean energy and electric devices powered by solar and wind, supplemented by reliable nuclear power.

The adoption of clean energies would have occurred naturally if it proved cost-effective. However, various studies project that a green transition would cost trillions of dollars per year globally.

Regulatory efforts to enforce these high costs have been attempted, but they have failed to mitigate the financial burden on low-income households, as detailed in the following pages. For decades, these households have borne the brunt of economic inequality, as highlighted in the free book referenced in the picture.

As a result, blue-collar workers have resisted efforts to combat global warming as long as they struggle to make ends meet and carbon regulations push them further into poverty. It is untenable for one half of the country to sacrifice for the other half, even in the name of addressing global warming. The lower middle class rejects the notion of their already low wages being further squeezed by carbon regulations while the upper-income segment reaps economic benefits, thrives in tech industries, and deploys robots that replace workers.

Solar and wind energy can't swiftly replace dirty power plants

The electricity produced from solar and wind sources, commonly referred as "*renewable energies*" or "*green energies*" may be virtually free as much as sunlight and wind are readily available and will never deplete. However, transitioning to a large-scale renewable energy infrastructure is challenging due to technical obstacles.

A primary challenge in scaling up solar and wind power is their low energy density, requiring numerous panels and turbines spread across large areas. Sunny deserts for solar farms or shorelines for floating turbines may be available, but both require costly infrastructure to transport the generated power to urban centers. Alternatively, decentralized production through rooftop solar panels is possible, but such individual installations lack the benefits of economies of scale.

A second challenge is the intermittent nature of solar and wind energy. Production is affected by nightfall or calm weather, and even seasonal variations, which can reduce output partially or entirely. This intermittency is a major concern for consumers, businesses, and essential services like hospitals, which may not have the financial resources to invest in backup batteries. In most cases, green power plants with battery storage cannot compete with fossil-fuel-based plants without subsidies.

Addressing the intermittency of solar and wind energy involves costly solutions:

• Super Grid: A "*Super Grid*" with high-power electrical interconnections utilizing HVDC (high-voltage direct current) lines over long distances can help mitigate intermittency. Such a grid could transport electricity generated by wind turbines in the Midwest to the sunny Southwest when solar generation drops after dark. At present, most electrical interconnections between cities or states remain insufficient.

• Pumped-storage hydroelectricity (PSH): PSH systems can pump water to a top tank during periods of maximum wind or sunlight and release it to generate electricity during peak demand or when wind and solar output is low. This system requires a suitable flat hilltop for the tank and a nearby water source to fill it.

• Compressed-air energy storage (CAES): CAES stores surplus electricity by compressing ambient air in an underground cavern or other storage medium. When demand rises, the pressurized air is heated and expanded through a turbine to generate electricity.

• Batteries and liquid hydrogen: Batteries and liquid hydrogen can store electricity and are also used in transportation technologies, as discussed in subsequent sections.

Implementing solar and wind energy solutions, including electrical storage, necessitates an increasing amount of metals for wind turbine generators, batteries, and the extension of the electrical grid to remote solar and wind power plants. The scarcity of raw materials may require the opening of new mines, recycling of used components, and the development of alternative alloys that do not rely on the rarest metals. These efforts will collectively contribute to a final cost estimated in the trillions of dollars.

Unlike renewable energy, fossil fuels can be easily stockpiled, with coal reserves and tanks filled with heating oil or liquid natural gas (as seen in the harbor of Barcelona) providing weeks of storage. This stored energy can fuel furnaces in winter or power air conditioning during heatwaves. The fossil fuel infrastructure, developed and paid for over the last century, continues to undercut clean energy solutions by providing reliable and readily available energy, with the ability to lower prices to maintain a competitive edge.

Other renewable energies: Small-scale only

Other renewable energy sources could generate electricity at a competitive market price and without CO_2 emissions. Unfortunately, they are not capable of being scaled up quickly and cost-effectively to replace the majority of dirty power plants.

• Hydroelectric dams are already in use for electricity production and flood prevention. The availability of suitable sites for new dams is limited, particularly in the US, restricting any expansion of hydroelectric energy.

• Biomass energy, derived from wood or organic waste, is commonly used for cooking and heating in developing countries. It also fuels power plants in Western countries. The downside is that biomass requires continuous harvesting, processing, and transportation of fuel—unlike solar panels or wind turbines. This makes biomass unsustainable in arid regions, unless future genetically modified plants can improve yields.

• Geothermal, wave, and tidal energy could one day serve as supplemental power sources. Pilot projects are underway, but achieving competitive costs will take time, especially since these resources are highly localized. For now, they can only diversify energy supply and help ease the intermittency of wind and solar power.

No country has yet embarked on a green transition that captures global attention by committing to a carbon-neutral economy within the coming decades. No government has developed an effective taxation and regulatory framework that avoids increasing unemployment and income inequalities.

Denmark, however, claims to be striving towards full renewable energy, even without international commitments. In 2011, Danish renewable energy accounted for 24% of total energy consumption (including electricity and petroleum). Around the same time, Denmark reduced its CO_2 emissions per capita by 15% compared to 1990 levels. By 2013, Denmark's per capita CO_2 emissions were less than half of those in the US. Denmark aims to be carbon-free by 2050 across all energy uses, including electricity, heating, and transportation.

Is Denmark the ideal model, with its successful economy, low unemployment, and leading performance in renewable energy? There are counterarguments:

• *Denmark depends on its neighbors' electricity when the wind isn't blowing or the sun isn't shining.*

• *Danish budgets invested in renewables (3.1% of GDP in 2011, compared to 0.3% for the US) was spent by the US on its military (around 4% of the US GDP, compared to 1.4% for Denmark's military), which protects Denmark for free under the US-NATO umbrella.*

Nuclear energy can't fully replace coal and natural gas in power generation

The existing *"nuclear fission"* technology (with uranium-based Generations II and III power plants) is the current technology in use in commercial nuclear power plants. These plants do not emit CO_2. However, they cannot be built in sufficient numbers to replace natural gas or coal-fired electricity on their own.

Three factors explained this limitation:

• Limited uranium reserves. "Known uranium reserves" are relatively scarce, even though uranium itself is widespread. These reserves consist of high-concentration deposits that are economically viable, both in dollar terms and in the energy required for extraction and refining. Such reserves would be depleted rapidly if Generation III nuclear power were expanded on a large scale. For example, a sixfold increase—enough to supply 66% of global electricity production (less than 14% of total global energy)—would exhaust them within 20 years.

• High construction costs. The construction of nuclear power plants is expensive and must be amortized over their typical 40-year lifespan to achieve an acceptable annual cost. This high annual cost helps explain the limited number of nuclear plants relative to known uranium reserves. An overly ambitious nuclear strategy could deplete these reserves before the plants' operational lifespans end, undermine profitability by leaving 40-year loans unpaid, and ultimately drive costs far above those of other energy sources.

• Skill shortage. Technicians, including welders and electricians, are in high demand across many sectors that compete with the nuclear industry, which has struggled to attract young talent over the past decades. This partly explains the continued development of Generation III power plants, which should help preserve the skills of nuclear professionals by providing continuous practical experience.

• Security concerns. The nuclear program raises security concerns regarding the potential for international proliferation of military nuclear capabilities from civilian nuclear technologies. The same technologies used to enrich uranium for civilian purposes (e.g., centrifuges that separate fissile isotope U-235 from the heavier U-238) can also be used to enrich uranium to levels suitable for military use (85%).

• Safety concerns. There are safety concerns related to nuclear melt-down accidents, as evidenced by the Chernobyl disaster in 1986 and the Fukushima disaster in 2011. The long-term safety of nuclear waste storage also remains a critical issue, requiring the construction of underground facilities where nuclear waste can be safely stored for thousands of years until it no longer emits dangerous radiation.

Next-Generation nuclear energy is not ready to replace fossil fuels

The upcoming *"nuclear Generation IV"* is not expected to provide cheap energy until approximately 2030, when the first commercial power plants are anticipated. This fission technology, which utilizes uranium and thorium, promises enhanced safety, a reduced dependency on limited known uranium reserves, and less waste that remains radioactive for shorter periods. Moreover, Generation IV reactors could potentially operate without new uranium mining, utilizing accumulated uranium waste from the 1950s to provide energy for the entire world for hundreds of years. Upon reprocessing, the resulting final waste would remain radioactive for only 300 years.

The latest *"nuclear fusion"* technology remains a distant prospect. Fusion aims to harness the immense heat from hydrogen reactions to generate steam, which can then produce electricity to power the planet and help combat global warming. Numerous projects are pursuing controlled hydrogen fusion, including international collaborations such as ITER, funded by major nations, and private ventures backed by figures like Bill Gates and Jeff Bezos. Their goal is to develop commercial nuclear fusion power plants in the near future. Realistically, however, mastering this "Holy Grail" of energy is more likely to occur toward the end of the century.

Clean electricity production must dramatically scale up

The aspiration for a predominantly electric future envisions a substantial increase in electricity's share of the global energy mix, potentially rising from the current 20% to approximately 90%. Clean fuels, such as biofuels, could account for the remaining 10%.

The envisioned near fivefold increase in electricity production must be achieved through *"clean energy,"* which includes both renewable and nuclear energy. Currently, clean energy constitutes only a fraction of total electricity generation, with renewable energy making up an even smaller proportion. This shift implies that the existing power plants, two-thirds of which run on coal and natural gas, would need to be replaced by clean energy power plants.

The conversion figures will have to include the population growth, and the rise of the middle class in countries such as China or India. Estimation of future electricity demand by 2050—always hard to predict accurately over the long term—can rise by 50% for the US, by 200% for China, or by 300% for India.

Fossil-fuel devices must switch to electricity or clean fuels

As clean energy ramps up, machinery and equipment that still rely on fossil fuels must transition to electrification or alternative clean fuels.

• Stationary devices with electrical wiring: The retrofitting and replacement of stationary machines and combustion appliances, such as furnaces and ovens, should transition to electrically-powered alternatives as these devices reach the end of their operational lifecycle. Plugging these devices into the electrical grid may require expanding the electrical cabling systems within and around buildings to ensure adequate capacity.

• Batteries for electricity without wire: Another challenge is electricity transmission for mobile equipment (cars, trucks, chainsaws...) not permanently connected to the electrical grid. Batteries are the primary energy storage solution for off-grid or unconnected devices.

Yet, batteries must improve on all fronts to win the energy vector race. First, advances in technology and mass production are essential to lower battery costs. Second, innovations in new metals and electrolytes must extend battery life cycles, reducing the need for costly replacements or recycling after a few years. Third, the development of smaller and lighter batteries is essential for powering vehicles over long distances. Fourth, fast-charging stations must be available everywhere for a long distance away from home. Fifth, cheaper materials must replace the rare cobalt, nickel or manganese, as mining represents a challenge in energy, cost, and safety.

• Hydrogen as energy vector for transport: The energy cost of liquid *"hydrogen"* may bar it from winning the battle with batteries for being the power-conveyor for the moving elements of the economy. Battery technology seems cheaper than *"hydrogen fuel cells"* filled with liquid hydrogen, which can generate electricity in a chemical reaction with oxygen to produce water. (Fuel cells are not rechargeable using electricity like batteries; they need a tank filled with a fuel.) Producing liquid hydrogen is inherently energy-intensive due to its two-step process: electrolysis, which splits water into hydrogen gas using electricity, followed by the compression and refrigeration of the gas into liquid hydrogen for storage. This liquefaction phase results in significant energy loss.

Despite these challenges, liquid hydrogen offers notable advantages: high energy density by weight, making it suitable for long-distance air travel; lower metal demand compared to batteries; straightforward storage in tanks; and the ability to absorb excess electricity generated from clean power plants.

• Biofuels: Derived from living organisms, such as oil extracted from plants and methane from biomass decomposition, biofuels like ethanol and biodiesel present a non-electric alternative that could complement an all-electric solution. Due to the current limitations and high costs associated with their production, biofuels can only serve as a supplement and are unlikely to power the entire economy.

• Solar fuels: Utilizing CO_2 from the air through artificial photosynthesis powered by sunlight, solar fuels, also known as electrofuels or e-fuels, offer a potential solution. These experimental fuels could be burned in engines, potentially providing a renewable energy source for the remaining gasoline-powered vehicles still in circulation.

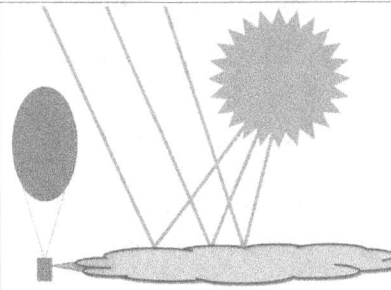

The necessary technologies are the not ready. The expertise to produce cheap clean energy and devices powered by electricity or other clean fuels isn't there yet. For this reason, the current approach of the Western world appears to be one of deferment, with a reliance on the future affordability of renewable energy and energy-efficient technologies driven by ongoing research and investment.

With this delay in mind, bringing down emissions by switching to clean energies may happen too late, as CO_2 can linger for centuries in the high atmosphere. Alternative technologies could mitigate GHG emissions already in the atmosphere:

*• CO_2 removal from the air with negative emissions technologies (NET)—also called carbon dioxide removal (CDR) technologies—could capture CO_2 and inject it into the ground. The technologies for capturing CO_2 include: green plants absorbing CO_2 and extracting it from these crops, ground installations sucking CO_2 from the air with the same (energy-voracious) technologies used in submarines, balloons in high altitude removing frozen CO_2, and finally capturing CO_2 out of the smokestacks of the coal-burning power plants before storing it underground with the so-called "**Clean Coal**" project.*

• Geoengineering technologies encompass "solar radiation management" with changes to the composition or color of oceans and clouds, with artificial cloud formation (as with a balloon in the picture), or with space mirrors to reflect solar energy away from the earth. These hypothetical technologies are deemed inexpensive, but they must undergo testing as they carry risks of unexpected side effects. Hopefully, the world won't have to go down this last path.

No, Borrowing Cannot Bankroll Everything

Splurging through borrowing to solve it all?

Given the pressing need to address climate change, could endless borrowing be justified to fund green projects? Shouldn't banks be compelled to extend generous loans at low interest rates, with repayment terms stretching across centuries? Wouldn't it make sense for governments to adopt such a financial strategy to promote social equity and provide long-term solutions to pressing challenges?

Alternatively, the government could bypass private banks and have the Treasury raise funds by issuing "*bonds*"—loan contracts that pay periodic interest. These bonds would be sold to the public in the "*bond market*," a network of brokers who buy and resell bonds. The "*Federal Reserve System*"—commonly known as the "*Fed*"—could step in and purchase large amounts of these bonds to stabilize the Treasury market, as it often does. Such funding methods were used during World War I, World War II, the 2008 financial crisis, and the 2020 COVID-19 crisis. At those times, Congress approved substantial borrowing to finance stimulus packages without raising taxes, supporting projects that created jobs. Isn't it time to embrace extensive borrowing in one form or another?

Borrowing like crazy leads to inflation

Borrowing multiplies money

Contemporary monetary creation evolved through centuries of financial trial and error, as illustrated in the following picture. Today, it begins with the requests of borrowers. To meet these requests, banks are authorized to create money "out of thin air" by crediting most of the loan amount to borrowers' accounts. In this sense, monetary creation is initiated by borrowers rather than solely by bankers' unilateral decisions. However, this process carries risks: if a borrower defaults, the bank must absorb the loss—typically by using profits earned from interest on other performing loans to cover the shortfall.

It is important to note that the money supply originates from borrowing through bank loans. Borrowers then spend this newly created money on goods, services, raw materials, machinery, and labor. These resources empower borrowers to produce, sell, keep some profits and finally pay back their loan. This process constitutes a critical aspect of the broader economic cycle, putting financial institutions at the core of the economy.

A short summary about "monetary creation":

For thousands of years, the ounce of gold or silver was the basis of money, with a ratio of roughly 15 ounces of silver equating to 1 ounce of gold. Monetary creation or "money supply" came from mining and coining precise fractions of ounces of silver or gold. Although banking did exist, its primary function was limited to loaning the precious coins in deposit at the bank. Banks could have 100 coins from depositors, and the same bank could loan 50 coins, whose depositors were unlikely to withdraw soon.

Around 1700, monetary creation started to stray away from mining gold and silver. At that time, bankers learned magically to loan 110 coins with only 100 coins in their vaults, which was a true monetary creation of 10 coins! How did they do it? In fact, borrowers would not withdraw 110 coins, but instead they would withdraw 110 coin-equivalents in the form of the new paper banknotes recently invented. Borrowers would accept withdrawing their loans in banknotes, because these banknotes were convertible into precious coins at the bank's counter. These banknotes could return for coin-conversion, but only after payment in a few days or even weeks, as customers would start trusting and keeping these banknotes. This trust enabled the bank to issue banknotes equivalent to 110% of its coin reserves in order to earn more interest.

Over the course of the 18th and 19th centuries, monetary creation has gradually shifted from minting gold or silver coins, to borrowing banknotes convertible into coins... until the suspension after 1930 of coin-convertibility in most countries.

Today, money is created through bank loans, as by everyone who has a credit card (as in the picture). Each time a credit card is used to pay for a purchase, money is created in this credit account. Of course, money is destroyed when the credit card account is paid back, but other credit card users will borrow simultaneously to sustain and potentially augment the overall money supply. For more detailed information, refer to the book "The History of Money for Understanding Economics," mentioned on the last page.

Money multiplication: Tempting and dangerous

Of course, rapid money multiplications have been attempted throughout history—whether through the debasement of coins, the printing of banknotes, or unrestrained borrowing—from Roman emperors to the 1970s and even today in corrupt countries. For centuries, demagogues have borrowed recklessly, either to cling to power or under the pretense of addressing global challenges.

In reality, a dramatic increase in money creation by governments—whether through a string of loans from private banks or through massive public loans from a central bank to its government—has never been a panacea for resolving economic problems. On the contrary, such endless borrowing has consistently disrupted the economy through inflation and, in some cases, has even doomed entire economies as they slid into hyperinflation.

If an immense treasure or even a mountain of gold would be found, could the government distribute gold ingots to the people and all the problems of global warming and inequality would be solved? Certainly not. In reality, the price of gold would simply collapse.

Similarly, if a vast amount of loans were coerced from banks, flooding the government coffers and people's pockets with endless dollars, it would not resolve issues such as climate change and even low wages. Instead, the value of money would collapse due to a phenomenon known as inflation or even hyperinflation.

In case of money dump in circulation: Prices spike

Excessive borrowing can dangerously expand the money supply. This uncontrolled borrowing multiplies banknotes, which are then used in payments by the government, corporations, and private borrowers. The likely outcome is a mechanical rise in prices that unfolds as follows:

- Circulation Surge: Money enters circulation as it is spent by corporations and individuals who borrow or draw from their savings. It then flows among suppliers, workers, civil servants, and retirees—who all become consumers. With cash in hand, these customers throng the stores.

• Inventory Depletion: Producers and sellers see their inventory decreasing. They can't replenish their stocks quickly due to production inertia, delivery delays, or a lack of trained workers. To preserve stock for their best customers, they look for other ways to adjust.

• Price Adjustments: With low inventory levels, neither producers nor sellers can satisfy every customer—even with alternative products or brands. They begin selling without offering the usual discounts, which effectively causes prices to rise. In modern retail chains with displayed prices, marketing departments also respond to low stock levels by canceling weekly promotions and increasing prices. If low inventories affect a wide range of products, a broad spectrum of prices will rise—if not all.

In summary, a rapid multiplication of money in circulation sets off a chain of events that increases all prices across every sector and retail environment.

Bargaining in Arab countries is very instructive. If one has any doubt about the price hike linked to expanding money supply, he can show the camel owner a bundle of banknotes before negotiating the price of the camel ride.

Prolonged price rises characterized as inflation

Prices continuously rise when producers see their capacity to restock goods consistently outstripped by consumer demand fueled by cash in hand. As money multiplication continues, prices increase month after month, year after year. This phenomenon of generalized and prolonged rise of prices is called "*inflation*" or sometimes "*price inflation.*"

It is important to specify that the surge of a single price does not define inflation. An isolated price may increase from occasional, climatic or seasonal factors, while a simultaneous decline in another price can offset the effect. Instead, inflation is the measure of the average rise of all prices across the entire spectrum of goods and services.

It should also be noted that a sudden panic can increase money in circulation when buyers empty their savings and rush to clear out store shelves. This general surge in prices is not considered inflation, as it is not persistent and prices may stabilize later on.

Lasting high inflation would drag the economy down

Savers, such as retirees or those with future spending targets, will see the purchasing power of their savings trimmed by inflation. They will realize it as their savings yields struggle to keep pace with the climbing prices of food, utilities or their dream purchase. They are rarely compensated by high interests when borrowing rules are lax, as it was the case during the 1970s. They will find themselves compelled to curtail their consumption of unessential goods and services.

Not all workers receive raises that keep pace with inflation, especially when job security concerns loom large—particularly in companies hurt by weak demand from savers. As a result, many cut back on spending, further worsening the economic outlook.

Corporations and businesses will grapple with the challenges posed by inflation, which creates uncertainty in future demand patterns due to dwindling savings. As a result, factories may reduce output and inventory to mitigate the risk of selling products at a loss due to possible weak demand. This cautious approach often involves furloughs and hiring freezes to align with scaled-back production.

Inflation's disproportionate impact on the poor

Inflation hits the lower middle class hardest. They face rising expenses and have limited financial resources to withstand persistent price increases, particularly in food and housing. Their savings lose value, while securing wage increases becomes more difficult—especially during an inflation-driven slowdown. As a result, many in this group are forced to cut back on spending, which can further weaken the economy.

The poorest individuals fare somewhat better, since their welfare benefits are indexed to inflation. But this support does not extend to the middle class, which earns too much to qualify for assistance yet still struggles with rising costs.

By contrast, the wealthy are better positioned to shield themselves from inflation. With access to financial expertise, they can invest in inflation-resistant assets such as gold, real estate, or stocks.

Inflation could feed on itself and get out of control

Borrowing let loose through accommodating interest rates and regulations to fix all the problems of the world would favor borrowers, as their repayments are eased by inflation. Borrowers could even borrow, buy, wait for inflation to drive up their value, resell at a higher price, pay back the fixed loan amount with its meager interests, while cashing in the price discrepancy between transactions. This borrowing on steroids, with a continual influx of new loans, would inject shot after shot of banknotes in circulation and worsen inflation.

Long-term investments are penalized by inflation, which makes forecasting of upcoming costs uncertain and demand of savers unsure. The least profitable projects end up being declined, as investors dread a repayment hit by climbing costs and shrinking demand. Instead, investors prefer unproductive placements such as real estate, stock market, or commodities.

At that point, the negative spillover of inflation begins to seriously derail the economy with job cuts of idle workers as a consequence of discontinuing low-return projects unable to keep up with inflation. Then, the risk exists for inflation to feed on itself with a dangerous spiral of always more banknotes, less output and less jobs.

In January 1922, Germany entered a period of "hyperinflation," marked by extremely rapid price increases. The money supply ballooned through borrowing, while the availability of goods paradoxically shrank. After all, why work hard to produce if savings could not be preserved at a stable value? As incentives to work collapsed, production shifted to meeting only short-term needs. National output fell sharply, and the entire country grew poorer. In the end, multiplying money only meant longer lines for food—and paying 45 million marks for a pound of butter. This episode underscores that real wealth lies in tangible goods, not in the symbolic illusion of paper banknotes.

Since the 1980s: Borrowing under surveillance

Containing money supply to curb inflation

The sobering experience of the 1970s, with its stubborn inflation, changed the minds of economists. They stopped believing that an economic slowdown should be countered with ever more borrowing and public spending, as had been done during World War II and the postwar era—especially since money could be created easily through borrowing after gold convertibility for the American public ended in 1934.

Economists came to assume that a major cause of economic slowdowns was inflation fueled by excessive borrowing. Implicitly, they accepted that output would normally remain strong, since workers were ready to roll up their sleeves and corporations were eager to expand production quickly to capture market share. Since then, this view has held significant sway among economists, who generally agree that inflation is, above all, a monetary phenomenon tied to loose borrowing rules.

With this shift in thinking, policymakers accepted that borrowing must be contained, even when pursued for worthy goals such as fighting global warming or funding welfare programs to reduce poverty. Strict oversight is essential to keep the money supply from spiraling out of control.

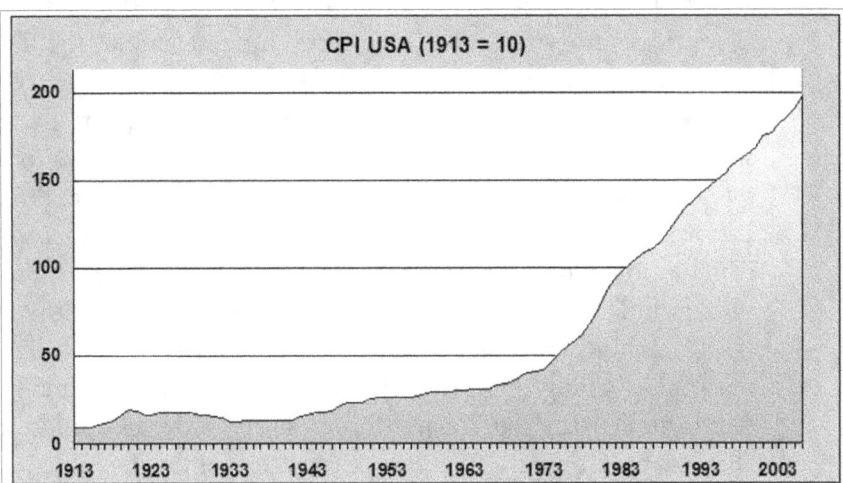

*In the 1970s, the US was confronted with an upswing in inflation (as visible in the picture with inflation measured by the Consumer Price Index). Inflation was a new phenomenon. People witnessed the purchasing power of their savings eroded by inflation. The unemployment rate was climbing. The economic growth was stuttering. The post-war economic policies—inspired by the economist John Keynes and known as "**Keynesianism**"—were challenged by inflation. The continuously low interest rates and recurrent public deficit to boost governmental spending were backfiring with inflation.*

*Around 1980, inflation became the main economic focus. The alternative ideas of the "**monetarist**" economists, spearheaded by the economist Milton Friedman, were finally taken seriously. Their monetarist ideas came to amend Keynesianism, with the central analysis that the government often triggers the economic instability, more than corporations inclined to grow their market shares, and not always overcautious as believed by Keynesianism.*

From then on, the strategy shifted from high-taxes-with-government-spending to tax-cuts-with-less-government, while targeting low inflation. In other words, the spending of the borrowing was entrusted to the private sector. It was hoped that money and borrowing in hands of people and corporations would lift the economy, not borrowing controlled by the government's bureaucracy.

Borrowing under the scrutiny of an independent Fed

In 1977, Congress revised the Federal Reserve's mandate to fight inflation, though it took several years before it was effectively implemented. The Fed is now charged with promoting maximum employment, stable prices, and moderate long-term interest rates. The Fed has different tools to comply with its mandate:

• The Fed must slow the pace of borrowing to regulate the money supply and ensure that inflation stays near 2% per year, as measured by the Consumer Price Index (CPI) published by the Bureau of Labor Statistics. To do so, the Fed aims at raising interest rates, which should discourage borrowing, limit the money supply and muzzle inflation. Specifically, the Fed influences short-term interest rates—technically called the short-term *"yield"*—on the bond market by selling or buying short-term bonds at a desired interest rate. The Fed has the dollars to buy, stash and resell bonds, as it is allowed by Congress to create money ex nihilo like any bank, as explained previously. The Fed's desired short-term rate will compel corporate bond sellers to compete with a similar interest rate if they want to find a buyer. Indirectly, all mid-term and long-term banking interest rates will align accordingly. Banks will be unable to offer loans at much higher interest rates than those available in the bond market, as other financial entities can issue bonds and use the proceeds to provide loans at competitive rates.

• The Fed may reduce its interest rates to encourage borrowing and sustain consumption during an economic slowdown. In case of a banking crisis, the Fed may even provide emergency loans to rescue institutions that did not trigger the crisis, but always with collateral assets left at the Fed. This helps to ensure that banks remain solvent and able to lend to businesses and consumers.

• The Fed must be impartial to support the economy. The Fed must maintain political neutrality and avoid using monetary policy to manipulate interest rates for partisan political purposes, and never helping one political party or another win an election. The *"Fed"* is an independent Central Bank, not fully controlled by the government. It is not permitted to lend money directly to the government. This is a common practice among Central Banks around the world, especially since credit facilities from Central Banks to governments have been banned in most countries since the 1980s. To ensure its neutrality, the Fed was granted relative independence from the government, with its board members elected for 14 years (thus, escaping a systematic demotion with each new US President), except for the President of the Board nominated for only 5 years. The Fed operates under a clear legal framework, which includes the obligation to reject funding for an overspending populist government.

Before considering a surge in borrowing, it is important to understand that banknotes are like certificates attesting of "rights-to-consume" that should only be granted after the completion of "efforts-to-produce."

Individuals can get an advance or a loan of rights-to-consume, provided they repay it soon. This is possible as long as others are saving their rights-to-consume for later and they keep producing more than they currently consume. Obviously, the volume of borrowed rights-to-consume must match the output of efforts-to-produce intended to be saved.

If a government, for populist reasons, forces the overissuance of these rights and their free distribution, merchants will inevitably observe an accelerated depletion of their inventories beyond their replenishment rate. Rapidly, the rights-to-consume would depreciate, mirroring the currency collapse of a failed state.

Only during a crisis can the government borrow and spend rights-to-consume when people are too scared to spend their own rights-to-consume. As the crisis subsides and confidence returns, this borrowing must be phased out so that individuals can once again rely on their own rights-to-consume.

The Treasury's borrowing on the bond market

To address the deficit between tax revenue and public expenditures, the Treasury can sell its bonds, but exclusively to the public of private corporations and private citizens within the "*bond market.*" This market is a network of brokers who buy and resell on behalf of a diverse clientele including individuals, corporations, banks, and foreign entities. It is important to note that private banks can purchase Treasury bonds, but they do so using funds from deposits, not from heavily regulated loan accounts that are credited with money out-of-thin-air.

The first reason for Treasury bonds is for banning bank loans credited with money out-of-thin-air from the Fed which must maintain its political impartiality. Such a method of public borrowing from the Fed would be equivalent to a bank loan out-of-thin-air, which is banned, as seen previously. In the same spirit, the Fed can only create money to engage in bond transactions on the open market—never directly with the Treasury—with the sole objective of ensuring economic stability. It is vital that the Fed refuses to shovel cash to the government's Treasury, in order to clamp down on distribution of free money before upcoming elections, even if this limitless funding stems from laudable goals, such as fighting global warming or mitigating inequalities. Any borrowing spree has inherent risks of economic destabilization. It cannot be overlooked.

The second reason for selling bonds is to enable the bond market to distinguish and reject junk bonds issued by an inept government. This mechanism ensures a layer of accountability and transparency, fostering a balanced economic landscape. It means that the bond market must have trust in the government to buy its Treasury bonds. The same happens for states, counties and cities selling their own municipal bonds. Obviously, the same is true for previous bond issues which can quickly lose value if a government suddenly changes its course toward insanity.

The rejection criteria of the lenders is based on an assessment considering three main elements:
- Risk of loan default: Lenders will examine the country's economic strategy and its prospective ability to fulfill its bond repayment obligations. Also, lenders pay scrupulous attention to a nation's level of indebtedness. This factor becomes paramount when a nation, already burdened by debt, is hit by a global crisis. Such an accident can severely diminish the country's tax revenue, rendering it incapable of meeting its interest obligations.

- Risk associated with the currency denomination of bonds: Another limit of borrowing is the chronic weakness of a foreign currency, often correlated with the recurrent elections of demagogic leaders. In this context, the bond market will be as vigilant as the currency market. The bond market may demand that bonds be issued in strong dollars or euros.

• The interest rate on the bonds: investors scrutinize the interest rate on bonds, comparing the yield with those of other bonds available in the market. In some instances, particular bonds must offer a much higher return than other bonds to compensate for the inherent risks.

Public deficits are tolerable if they don't impede growth

A small amount of public borrowing is built into most government budgets. A public deficit is generally acceptable if it amounts to only a few percent of "*GDP*" (Gross Domestic Product). GDP represents the total income of a nation and reflects its capacity to repay debt. It is calculated by summing consumption, investment, government spending, and net exports.

An annual deficit smaller than the rate of annual GDP growth would even imply a declining debt-to-GDP ratio. For example, a 2% public deficit coupled with 3% growth results in a shrinking debt burden relative to output. For this reason, GDP growth serves as a key indicator of economic health and as a measure of the sustainability of public debt.

Governments should avoid expanding borrowing beyond the generally sustainable deficit level of 2–3% of GDP, except in times of crisis. During such crises, borrowing is preferable to raising taxes, since higher taxes in a downturn discourage spending and investment, weakening the economy and delaying recovery. By contrast, a faster recovery increases fiscal revenues sooner and reduces the deficit more quickly than if the crisis were prolonged.

Finally, a permanent large-scale public deficit should never be allowed, even with the aim of financing climate policies, creating jobs or even building hospitals and schools. Such a policy would only expand bureaucracy and generate inflationary pressures that could derail the economy.

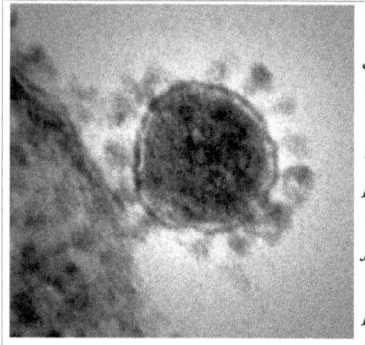

Yes, the government must step in during emergencies like the Covid crisis, but the same recipe can't fund a flurry of public projects.

During the Covid lockdown, emergency funding helped the people and businesses to stay afloat by paying their bills, and later by supporting the recovery. This funding didn't last for more than a few months.

By contrast, large-scale borrowing to fund public projects and create good-paying jobs for everyone was tried during the 1960s and 1970s— not just for a few months, but for decades. It ultimately failed, as persistent inflation punished everyone.

Risk of crowding-out effect from public deficits

Another consequence of the public deficit happens within the financial markets. To cover its deficit, the government monopolizes the cheapest lending, taking it away from the private sector. This phenomenon is referred to as the so-called *"crowding-out effect,"* which is characterized by numerous borrowers competing for cheap loans. Ineluctably, interest rates have to rise when affordable lending options become depleted.

This crowding-out adversely affects corporations. Their profits are squeezed by higher interest expenses and by the loss of income from secondary investments that become unprofitable under elevated rates. With reduced corporate output, the crowding-out effect tends to increase inflationary pressures, even though higher interest rates also reduce consumer spending.

The resulting inflationary tensions force the Fed to raise interest rates to contain the price rise, in order to comply with its current mandate. Since the 1980s, the annoyance of the 1970-style inflation has been de-facto replaced by the grinding of high interest rates induced by the Fed, which can add up on top of the crowding-out effect on interest rates resulting from the deep public deficit.

If the government runs a persistent deficit to "save the world," the Fed would have to stay the course, keeping politically neutral and raising interest rates. That path would almost certainly bring higher unemployment and an economic slump, caused by crippling interest rates caused by the government's expansive borrowing. This downturn would come even if inflation stayed under control.

Nowadays, the economic consensus holds that excessive government intervention and large public deficits, financed through taxation and borrowing, can drain resources from corporations and stifle entrepreneurial spirit as well as the individual initiative of workers. Nimble capitalist enterprises, motivated by the need to enhance efficiency and reduce costs, is the only effective path to bolster the Treasury's revenue through taxation.

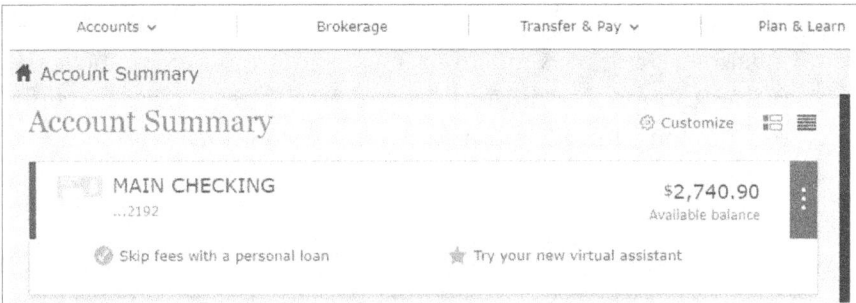

The money sitting in deposit accounts is not pilling in the bank's vault. While the bank owes the account holder the deposited funds, it does not keep all that money on hand. Most of it is typically invested in corporate or Treasury bonds or lent out to other customers. In the end, only a small fraction of the money in checking or savings accounts is held in the bank's vault to accommodate customer cash withdrawal requests.

Any additional sale of Treasury bonds cannot rely on money that banks do not physically hold; it can only draw on existing cash reserves held by private investors. As a result, Treasury bonds must offer competitive interest rates to attract that capital, which may, in turn, reduce the funds available for other corporate investments.

The money illusion

It is imperative to reiterate that irresponsible borrowing is only blessed by fools suffering from *"money illusion"* when they view wealth and income in nominal money value, without taking into account the real value adjusted for inflation.

Worse, fully-fledged demagogy of a misguided government borrowing endlessly from its central bank could fuel hyperinflation.

This is particularly dramatic in countries such as in Germany in the 1920s, Argentina in the 1970s or Zimbabwe in the late 2000s.

This money illusion can be attributed to inadequate financial education among the public, the media, and even intellectuals who are easily dazzled by stacks of banknotes as a panacea. This illusion fosters the rise of populists who promise unlimited borrowing as a solution to global problems. The spread of such monetary misconceptions is extremely dangerous and can have far-reaching consequences.

In reality, the government can't compel banks to pay with the money that they don't have, in order to provide well-paid jobs that don't exist yet. The weekly wages would be spent way before any slow output, which would pressure prices upward and hit the economy with inflation. Dangerous inflationary pressure from money shoveled to the masses can severely disrupt the economy. These tactics certainly won't provide food for all, green tech for a carbon-free world and military protection for allies. This inept solution would only level down society at the poorest bottom.

Prior to considering reckless private or public borrowing, one must understand that money is like a number, a counter or a fuel gauge (as in the picture). In this sense, people must effectively fill the tank before they can drive as long as the fuel gauge indicates that there is gasoline in the tank.

Excessive borrowing to allow the distribution of free dollars is like tampering with the gauge to indicate a full tank without producing gasoline and refilling the car. Despite the gauge indicating a full tank, the car won't go as far as expected. The amount of gasoline is determined by the many hours of numerous hardworking people in oil wells all the way to replenishing gas stations, not by manipulating the fuel gauge with a populist decree..

No, Overtaxing High Incomes Is Not a Panacea

Jacking up taxes on high wages and corporate profits?

Some propose a straightforward solution for the government to fund projects targeting climate change and social inequalities: increasing tax rates on affluent individuals and their corporations. This argument advocates for government intervention to levy higher taxes on these entities, with the aim of funding infrastructure, expanding healthcare facilities, and creating well-paid jobs. This approach is viewed as a counterbalance to the private sector's inadequacies in addressing environmental cleanup and low wages.

After all, higher tax rates were prevalent during the post-war period and the economy was humming with higher wages. Shouldn't the people unite to impose a fair taxation system to finance a full-employment economy with lower inequalities? Isn't it a no-brainer to demand a tax rate increase, which is blocked by the greedy rich hoarding their cash and conspiring with their lobbyists in Washington?

Robin Hood for President? Just raise all tax rates on the rich and on their corporations, then the government can spend, create jobs, and solve it all?

Yes, Robin Hood could have helped his people by stealing the coins hoarded by the greedy Rich. In the medieval period, the circulation of precious coins was crucial for economic transactions, but there was a shortage of gold and silver for coinage due to the scarcity of mines.

Today, dollars deposited in savings accounts are not idle; they generate additional dollars through loans and investments in production, which must precede consumption. Therefore, high tax rates can deplete funds intended for new ventures, and a dollar taxed from the wealthy does not necessarily translate into jobs or affordable goods for the poor.

It is essential to recognize that advancements such as longer life expectancy and lower child mortality, have resulted from private investments in producing essential goods like soap and water pipes. Redirecting funds from investments in competitive corporations to inefficient government-run public projects risks outcomes similar to those of communist regimes in Russia and China during the 20th century.

Heavy taxation: A political threat

A first principle of taxation is the necessity of moderation. Individuals must retain sufficient private resources to own independent media outlets, hire lawyers or bodyguards, and enjoy the leisure needed to express themselves. This right, which safeguards against potential government overreach, is an essential component of historical charters aimed at curbing despotism, such as the Magna Carta (1215), the US Constitution (1787), and the Universal Declaration of Human Rights (1948), further reinforced by the International Covenant on Civil and Political Rights (1966).

With abusive taxation, an authoritarian faction—even if representing the majority—could silence dissent. Nothing is easier than forcing political opponents into the harsh labor of subsistence. Election rigging is then legitimized by state-controlled media muzzled by the ruling council. Finally, an ambitious dictator is free to eliminate rivals through sham lawsuits or orchestrated accidents.

In this sense, abusive taxation—even in the name of helping the poor or saving the planet from global warming—is both pernicious and specious. History has repeatedly shown that regimes replacing private initiative with state bureaucracies have failed economically, impoverished many, and too often descended into totalitarianism.

Better a communist government closely monitored by the people united, instead of omnipotent private corporations responsible for low wages, inequality, even global warming and pollution?

Warning: past experiments have shown many risks associated with communist regimes.

Communism has a poor record for improving people's lives, let alone of protecting the environment. Soviet wealth was all in the hands of the communist elite, not the people. China isn't cleaner with cities such as Beijing having some of the most polluted air on the planet or much more equal, only surmounting extreme poverty by allowing capitalism around Shenzhen or Shanghai.

In front of the poor results, benevolent politicians tend to be overthrown by ruthless challengers in order to "save" the regime (e.g., as these two in the picture who jailed their rivals). These dictators prioritize maintaining their grip on power over addressing issues like curbing inequalities or global warming. They are more likely to hide the true figures of poverty or GHG emissions, suppress free press, and quell public dissent.

High taxes and the stagflation of the 1970s

High tax rates on incomes were already tried in the past, notably during the 1950s. During this period, the marginal income tax rate reached 91% under the US federal income tax, and the corporate tax rate exceeded 50%. This resulted in an effective tax rate of approximately 42% for the wealthiest taxpayers, who could compensate themselves with stocks or dividends, optimizing for lower tax rates and potential deductions. These tax rates were among the highest in historical records.

This strategy began to backfire in the late 1960s and 1970s, a period marked by increased government spending driven by factors such as the Vietnam War, the Apollo space program, and President Johnson's

"Great Society" welfare programs. The adverse long-term economic consequences of inflated tax rates became evident during this time. The high tax rates proved counterproductive for several underlying reasons:

- Business relocation: People move their business to countries with more favorable tax environments or engage in legal tax-exempt schemes, effectively reducing the domestic tax base.

- Shift to the Underground Economy: People conceal their business in the underground economy, perhaps receiving unemployment checks while working in the underground economy.

- Reduced Consumer Spending: Taxation lowers workers' disposable income, limiting spending mainly to everyday staples and potentially reducing corporate output and employment in more sophisticated goods and services.

- Investment Impediment: Punishing taxation reduces the capital available to both wealthy and middle-class individuals for investment in new ventures. Such investments are crucial for job creation and for providing goods and services to the people.

High taxes, therefore, can impede work, consumption, investment, and innovation by diverting funds away from the productive purposes that fuel economic growth. This reduction in the production of goods and services contributed to inflation, as the ratio of money over goods increases. Attempts by the government to stimulate the economy through escalating deficit spending further exacerbated inflation, as discussed in the previous chapter. This situation culminated in a scenario where, as economists often describe, an excess of money was chasing a limited supply of goods, intensifying a vicious circle of inflationary pressures and economic slowdown.

The 1970s marked the culmination of a period known as "*stagflation*," characterized by economic stagnation coupled with inflation. This era reached a critical point when unemployment levels escalated to what was termed "mass unemployment." These economic challenges served as a valuable lesson for policy makers. There is now a broad recognition that excessive taxation proved ineffective in this past experiment. Many experts agree that this approach is unlikely to yield positive results in the future and poses a risk to the principles of democracy.

Contrary to popular belief, the government does not itself perform miracles such as building roads or feeding the poor. Instead, its role is largely fiscal: it collects funds from individuals and corporations and channels those resources to the private sector to carry out projects and services. For example, the construction of roads, dams, and military equipment is typically outsourced to private corporations through a public bidding process, which fosters competition. Similarly, in welfare programs, the government rarely provides goods or services directly. Instead, recipients of programs like food stamps or Medicare use their handouts to purchase what they need from private providers, retaining the freedom to choose their suppliers.

The government's involvement in the management of public services is concentrated in sectors where the presence of private corporations might not align with the public's best interest. Only then, the government establishes monopolistic entities, which are operated by civil servants. These entities function within a framework where operational guidelines, pricing structures, and regulatory standards are determined by the bureaucratic processes of local, state, or federal legislative bodies. Notable examples of such government-operated sectors include K-12 education, the armed forces, police departments, and public utilities.

In the end, the government relies on the private sector to provide products and services to the public. This practice is considered more efficient compared to historical instances of extensive governmental control, such as those observed in the USSR and during the regulatory excesses of the 1970s.

Since 1980, cutting tax rates for more(!) fiscal revenues

The stagflation and mass unemployment of the 1970s catalyzed a shift in tax policy and economic thought. This economic failure paved the way for the acceptance of an alternative economic perspective.

By around 1980, new economic theories emerged to challenge the 1970s-style taxation of the wealthy. They argued that such high taxation inadvertently harmed the most vulnerable by depriving them of work. The resulting reduction in private investment—siphoned away by the IRS—hindered the creation of new enterprises and slowed economic growth. Over time, this dynamic could also reduce tax revenues, limiting the government's ability to effectively fund essential services such as education and welfare.

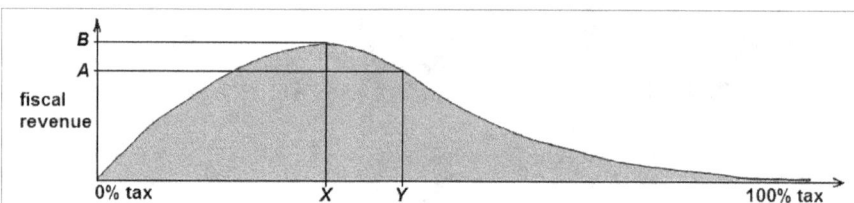

*Higher tax rates can bring less income to the government, not more! The economist Arthur Laffer illustrated it with his "**Laffer curve**":*

• On the left, at 0% tax rate, tax revenue is obviously zero. As the tax rate increases from this point, government revenue also begins to rise—a seemingly straightforward correlation.

• On the right, at a 100% tax rate, no one works intensely—except for Stakhanovites or model workers—since all wages are collected and redistributed by distant bureaucracies, with no regard for individual productivity. As a result, production falls to Stalinist levels as workers lose motivation and investors withdraw. At the same time, tax revenues collapse.

• To join both ends of the curve, the rising tendency on the left has to curb beyond a certain point. It happens when taxation becomes excessive, discouraging work, deterring investments, and fueling the underground economy. The curve is then flattening before decreasing with taxes starved by plunging profits and discouraging post-tax wages.

According to this curve, any tax percentage higher than the top of the curve (X) means that a tax cut—instead of a rate hike(!)—is counter-intuitively required to increase tax incomes! Yet, lowering the tax rate from Y to X will increase fiscal revenues from A to B only after a few years, because it takes time for investments and work motivation to come back. In the short term, a tax rate hike will bring more immediate revenue to the government.

Since the 1980s, the implementation of tax cuts has helped the economy recover from recurrent downturns. Despite ongoing challenges like persistent unemployment and wage stagnation in certain sectors, these fiscal policy adjustments have played a key role in revitalizing the economy.

Cutting tax rates to stem the economic crisis

To overcome the economic crisis of the 1970s, President Reagan signed laws to cut federal income taxation from a maximum tax rate of 70% to 50% with the Economic Recovery Tax Act of 1981, and then cut it down to 28% with the Tax Reform Act of 1986. Subsequent years saw fluctuations in the maximum tax rate from the 1990s to the 2020s, influenced by the prevailing majority in Congress. Despite these changes, the tax rates have not reverted to the peak levels experienced in the 1970s.

The primary objective of the tax cuts was to stimulate private investment. By increasing net income, individuals were encouraged to invest in financial markets, such as purchasing stocks on Wall Street, or to allocate funds into local businesses and startups. This policy enabled not only the wealthy but also the middle class to invest the additional income retained after taxation.

Furthermore, the tax cuts were anticipated to boost consumer spending, particularly among the lower income groups, who tend to have a higher propensity to spend. This contrasted with the upper classes, who generally maintained consistent consumption levels. Illustrative of this approach, the lowest bracket of the federal tax rate was reduced from 14% to 11% in 1981, a move specifically targeted to increase disposable income and stimulate spending among those in the lower income brackets.

After 1982, the economy started to recover. It was the rise of "supply-side economics," with its emphasis on the production of goods, moving away from the constraints of high tax rates, ineffective regulations, and prevailing inflation. In this climate, corporations found it easier to secure financing, employ workers, and market their products to the middle class. The strategy relied on the middle class being able to make purchases with their incomes, thus circumventing the challenges of unemployment and inflation prevalent in the 1970s. Despite the crises of 1991, 2001, and 2008, this supply-side approach has continued to dominate economic policy.

Cutting tax rates on capital gains for a new economy

Another response to the economic challenges of the 1970s was a series of successive reductions in capital gains tax rates under the administrations of Presidents Carter, Reagan, and Clinton. These tax cuts, implemented in 1978, 1981, and 1997, proved economically beneficial, particularly evident in the growth of the 1980s and 1990s. They stimulated investments in startups, facilitated through venture capital and Initial Public Offerings ("*IPOs*") in stock markets such as the NYSE and NASDAQ.

The lower tax rates of the 1980s and 1990s were instrumental in transitioning the economy away from traditional industries, paving the way for the emergence of a new economic landscape in the US. This shift not only revitalized the domestic economy but also had an impact internationally, with the European Union, among others, benefiting from the resultant boost in productivity and economic growth. These developments underscore the far-reaching implications of tax policies on the economy.

The recovery has not lifted low wages

After 1982, the economy halted its decline and began recovering in most sectors. However, this period has been marked by a persistent stagnation in middle-class wages. The situation is more pronounced for low-income earners, whose wages have actually decreased when adjusted for inflation. This decline can be attributed to factors such as the increased use of robotics, the influx of cheaper imports, and the relocation of manufacturing to foreign countries. Only the highest wages, particularly of those involved in high-tech products, have increased over these decades.

Economists are puzzled by this wage stagnation, especially when compared to the wage growth observed in previous periods of economic recovery. They can't explain how a tightening unemployment hasn't led to a wage increase. They can only confess lacking data to investigate the root causes among the potential culprits.

There is also growing concern among some economists that the tax cuts may have inadvertently contributed to the rise of a new high-tech economy that displaces workers and exerts downward pressure on low-skill wages. The rise of artificial intelligence and self-driving vehicles could potentially perpetuate the stagnation of low-skill wages indefinitely.

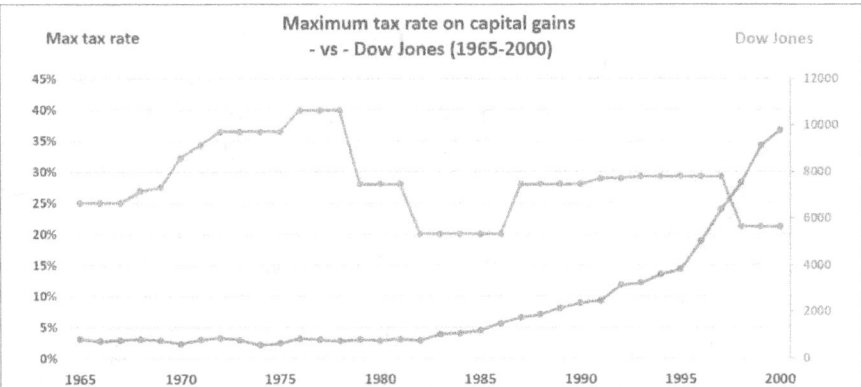

Lower tax rates allow venture capitalists and middle-class wage earners to retain more of their income. Much of this money is invested or reinvested into startups or stock market IPOs, though a portion may be spent on luxury goods. Such funding is vital for tech ventures, since banks are often reluctant to lend to young entrepreneurs with revolutionary ideas. Likewise, governments hesitate to back high-risk startups because their high failure rates—around 90%—could trigger political backlash.

The surge of the stock market, fueled by these dynamics, has attracted increased investment and a higher number of IPOs, thereby financing the burgeoning tech economy, with startups growing into tech giants, such as Genentech, Google or Amazon. This growth has also indirectly benefited the US Treasury, as evidenced by increased tax revenues from capital gains following each of the tax cuts in 1978, 1981, and 1997.

The downside was that the expansion of the stock market increased the wealth of the richest individuals, creating a disparity in wealth distribution. Concurrently, although unemployment rates decreased, there was a notable absence of wage growth for low-income workers. This growing economic inequality has become a source of dissatisfaction across the nation.

A comeback of high tax rates won't fix global warming or inequality

Ignoring the failures of the past, a radical government might choose to sharply raise all tax rates. Such a high-tax strategy would reduce the earnings of the wealthy, but it would not create large numbers of jobs, possibly green jobs, under government direction. Any increase in tax revenue would be short-lived, since it would never match the productive investments that might have been made with the confiscated money. Instead, it would produce politicized spending rather than sound investments—a pattern that has often fueled inflation, damaging the economy and long-term tax revenues. At best, it could recreate the stagflation of the 1970s; at worst, it could resemble the stagnation of the Soviet Union.

Such a high-tax strategy would disproportionately hurt the poor by slowing the economy and increasing unemployment. It would achieve the opposite of its intended effect. It would only deepen inequality between political elites and the masses of the poor. History shows that taxation alone cannot solve social problems; more often, it produces greater poverty and political instability.

To reduce poverty, it is better to cap tax rates at today's moderate levels. Ideally, this approach will remain the norm. Variations in these rates should stay small—perhaps rising slightly when Congress leans left or falling modestly when the right holds sway. Overall, these limited fluctuations within capped rates can be expected to provide the Treasury with a stable stream of revenue.

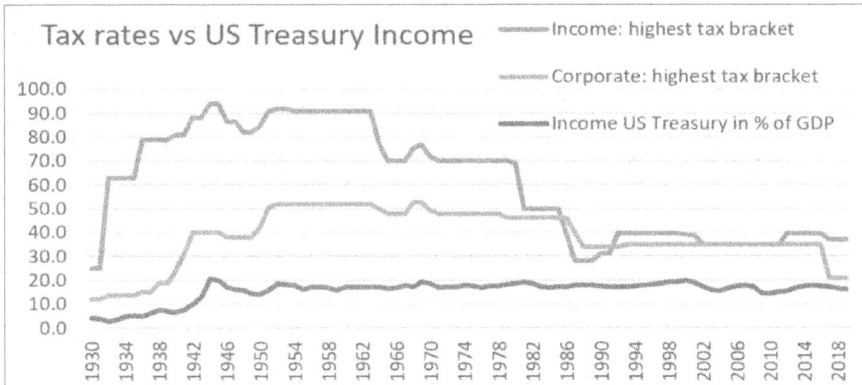

*High tax rates never made the US Treasury much richer in the past. The "**effective tax rate**"—the actual percentage of income paid by individuals and corporations—has not been much higher than it is today, averaging around 20% of GDP. It is therefore inaccurate to suggest that the postwar economic expansion occurred despite high tax rates, or that the lower tax rates of the 1980s led to reduced federal revenue.*

The relatively low tax collections of the 1950s and 1960s may have been partly due to tax avoidance and the use of exemptions. However, there should be no rush to eliminate all deductions and exemptions, treating them merely as loopholes. Many tax breaks play a critical role in encouraging risk-taking and innovation. Such incentives can enhance skills and expertise across fields from healthcare to defense, create jobs, and ultimately increase future tax revenues. Raising tax rates without preserving deductions could be counterproductive. Such measures risk job losses and widespread impoverishment by shifting focus from productive private enterprise to bureaucratic management. Industry leaders could be replaced by less efficient government appointees, hindering economic growth and innovation—ultimately harming everyone.

No, a Wealth Tax Won't Fund the Green Transition

Congress should just pass a new wealth tax, right?

There is a prevalent view that the very rich could reasonably be subject to increased taxation. Advocates of this approach argue that Congress should implement a new wealth tax, when income tax rates can't go much higher as learned since the 1970s. The argument behind this proposition is that it would empower the government to create well-paid jobs and fund solutions to all the problems of the world. Following this perspective, Congress must impose a wealth tax to address the situation.

Oxfam 2024: "billionaires are $3.3 trillion richer than they were in 2020"

Many sensational newspaper headlines imply that the wealthy earn trillions and that solving the world's problems is straightforward. In reality, most of this wealth is not liquid cash but is tied up in corporate shares valued according to the latest Wall Street quotations. Converting such wealth into cash on a large scale is highly impractical. If the wealthy were forced to sell large numbers of shares to pay a punitive tax, the lack of suffi-cient buyers could trigger a collapse in share prices. This situation would resemble a game of musical chairs, with wealthy individuals unable to hold all the shares and only low-income individuals to purchase them with their limited savings. Such a collapse would make it impossible to raise the necessary funds to pay the taxes on wealth. In the worst-case scenario, these punitive measures against the wealthy could echo the Russian deku-lakization of the post-1917 era, which led to widespread economic and social upheaval.

The cash of the rich is gone—tied up in loans or investments

A major misconception is the belief that the super-rich sit on piles of cash. In reality, their cash is largely gone, tied up in investments that contribute to economic growth. Much of this wealth has been allocated to acquiring corporate shares that yield dividends or government bonds that pay interest. Their investments also extend to real estate, building housing complexes and generating rental income. Some funds may also have been used to purchase assets such as gold ingots, seen as a hedge against currency devaluation. Only a small amount of cash remains in checking accounts, and even this typically circulates through the banking system, where deposits are used by banks to purchase bonds or extend loans.

Altogether, the assets of the wealthy are typically in the form of debt instruments, rather than hard cash. This composition makes it challenging to tax this wealth for funding infrastructure projects, educational initiatives, or green energy ventures. To pay a substantial wealth tax, these assets would need to be converted into cash before the tax deadline. This process, involving the large-scale liquidation of debt instruments, is not straightforward, far from it.

A wealth tax could still be applied to the remaining cash assets stored in investment and banking accounts. However, it is important to consider that this cash has already been taxed, either through income tax or capital gains tax. Furthermore, cash held in investment or banking accounts is often already loaned out through the bond market, money markets, Certificates of Deposit, or other financial instruments.

Is it the greedy rich (as guilty as in Bruegel's painting of the seven deadly sins) who are lobbying politicians to reject a wealth tax, which could fund green projects and job creation with good wages and solve it all?

No, not quite. The proposition that plundering the rich's wealth valued in billions of dollars would single-handedly resolve all societal issues is overly simplistic and does not fully grasp the true nature of economic realities.

The delusion lies in equating one dollar in wealth with one dollar in liquid cash or with one dollar in tangible output like bread. In reality, the cash was long ago invested in assets like machinery in exchange for a debt instrument. This resulting debt-title valued in dollars is not equal to the dollars' worth of bread in practical terms. They are valued the same in monetary units, but they are not interchangeable. The dollar serves merely as a unit of measurement for value, not value itself. To increase output, such as bread production, the focus should be on expanding arable land and improving crop yields, rather than attempting to extract value from non-liquid assets like machinery.

The conversion of assets such as debt instruments, or machinery into liquid cash necessitates their sale in the market. This process can be undertaken at will but is not feasible for rapid, large-scale liquidation, especially under the constraint of a wealth tax. The scenario where wealthy individuals are compelled to sell their assets, all valued in dollars, is impractical, as the rich cannot be a seller and buyer at the same time to accumulate cash for tax obligations. Moreover, the poor cannot participate as buyers due to their limited cash savings.

The misconception about the nature of wealth is prevalent among journalists and politicians. Wealth, which can be measured by aggregating the dollar value of various assets, must not be mistaken for liquid cash or essential commodities like food. The process of converting these assets into cash or necessary goods is neither direct nor immediate. Misinterpreting these disparate financial figures can confuse the public and does little to advance practical solutions to fundamental needs. This understanding is essential for accurately assessing economic resources and their potential impact on society.

Non-cash assets are difficult to tax

A wealth tax would require taxpayers to self-report their wealth until the administration develops a system for verifying the assets of millions of citizens.

The valuation of these assets should align with their current market value. For publicly traded stocks, a standard valuation method, such as the "200-day moving average" could be used, acknowledging the inherent volatility in stock market valuations. For privately held stocks, the valuation could be based on the dividends distributed over recent years. A similar approach, focusing on yield, would be applicable for the assessment of other types of assets, ensuring a consistent and fair evaluation methodology.

Not too fast, then! Implementing a 2% wealth tax could have significant economic implications. Such taxation could reduce risk-taking among investors, as the inability to offset losses with after-tax gains may discourage investment in future growth. Over time, this could harm the broader economy and even reduce government tax revenues, as suggested by the principles of the Laffer Curve.

A high wealth tax is unrealistic

A careful analysis is required when considering the implementation of a high wealth tax, such as the annual rate of over 3–4% proposed by some policymakers. Taxpayers would not be able to cover such a tax solely from dividends, since the average after-tax yield on stock dividends is typically only 1–2% of the stock's value in an average year. These taxpayers would need to sell portions of their stocks or bonds to meet their tax obligations. This raises the question of who would buy those assets.

Other wealthy individuals would not be likely buyers, since they too would be under pressure to sell assets to meet the same tax requirements. The wealthy cannot all buy and sell simultaneously to raise cash for taxes—it simply does not make sense. Nor could they realistically borrow funds to pay the tax, as banks would hesitate to issue such loans knowing that borrowers would struggle to find buyers with sufficient cash to purchase the assets.

The middle class is unlikely to fill this gap, since the average household has limited cash reserves. Most people's liquid assets, such as savings, are far smaller than their non-liquid assets, like the value of their homes.

In this scenario, there is a real risk of a downward spiral in stock prices due to a shortage of buyers. Because the majority of the stock market is owned by the affluent, a collective rush to sell could trigger a market crash. Even the super-rich might struggle to sell assets at reasonable prices to raise the cash needed to pay the tax. In extreme cases, this could prompt wealthy individuals to relocate to countries without a wealth tax to avoid bankruptcy in the United States.

Cash constitutes only a small portion of total assets. According to Federal Reserve data, the total cash supply, represented by the monetary aggregate M2, was approximately 15 trillion dollars in 2019. In comparison, the total asset valuation on Wall Street was about 30 trillion dollars as of 2018, as reported by the World Bank. This figure does not even include the stocks of corporations not listed on Wall Street, Treasury bonds, or gold ingots.

Given that the top 1% of wealth holders own a significant portion of Wall Street's stocks and bonds, imposing a 5% wealth tax on them would necessitate mobilizing a considerable amount of cash, possibly amounting to trillions of dollars, for the repurchase of these assets. Such a large-scale mobilization of cash could result in reduced cash availability for the general population to purchase goods and services, potentially impacting the overall economy.

Therefore, the idea of taxing non-cash assets (which are valued in dollars but are not actual cash) and distributing the proceeds as free cash to the people fails to account for the practical challenges associated with liquidating non-cash assets and the potential economic repercussions of such actions.

Asset confiscation will not revive the economy

Instead of direct cash payments to satisfy a high wealth tax, an alternative approach could involve the government confiscating a certain percentage of stocks, such as 1 out of every 10 shares. This strategy would avoid the need for problematic cash payments from the wealthy to the Treasury, thereby circumventing issues related to insufficient market liquidity to purchase the shares.

This system would, over time, nationalize corporations as the government accumulated shares through years of stock-based tax payments. The result would be a bureaucratic command economy, with corporations increasingly managed by government officials, whose decisions are influenced more by union pressures and social demands than by market competition and customer needs. Historically, governments have shown a poor track record in corporate management. Such centralized control could reduce profitability, hinder reinvestment in productive assets, and ultimately diminish economic output. The consequences might include lower sales, fewer jobs, a general decline in economic well-being, and an increasingly authoritarian, state-directed economy.

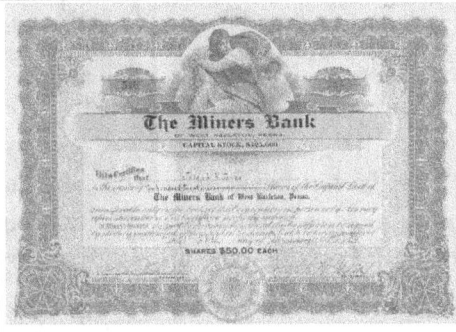

The rich don't sit on a pile of cash, but on a pile of financial securities—such as shares and debt instruments (as in the picture). In other words, the rich "only" own the means of production, not the output, which is mostly consumed by the people. And, the people want the output, not necessarily owning the means of production. The former may be owned by a few, but only the latter can be consumed by everyone through purchase in dollars. And no, the former can't be converted into the latter with a magic wand, even if they are both valued in dollars. It results that the government can never tax the rich from the cash that they don't have and spend it to solve all the problems of the world.

*The rich don't earn large amounts of cash year after year; rather, they see the market value of their assets rise. This misunderstanding can be seen as an advanced form of the money illusion, evolving into what can be termed a "**money delusion**," where wealth is inaccurately perceived as readily available cash. This view disregards the complexities involved in converting non-liquid assets to cash. Such oversimplifications create a distorted view of wealth, leading to impractical taxation policies, which scrape together only small amounts of cash for short-term, demagogic spending—at the dangerous expense of long-term investment. This money delusion is akin to the medieval perception of wealth as gold or silver coins, when such coins were scarce. Those who hold this view obsessively believe that confiscating imaginary hoards of gold and silver can resolve all the world's problems.*

Furthermore, individuals affected by the money illusion often believe that simply throwing money at a problem will solve it. These advocates have pushed for generous welfare programs since President Johnson's Great Society, yet such programs have not resolved the underlying issues. Many even argue that they backfired—fostering idleness, boredom, drug abuse, and crime. Effective solutions require more than just financial resources; they demand personal responsibility and sustained hard work.

Switzerland: Wealth tax success in a low-tax country

Switzerland shows that a wealth tax can be implemented effectively, as evidenced by its long-standing system. The tax is levied at a rate of less than 1% annually, striking a balance between revenue generation and maintaining a moderate burden. While Switzerland does impose a wealth tax, it is important to note that the country's overall tax burden —its "**tax-to-GDP ratio**" measured by international agencies—is comparable to that of the US and relatively low compared with typical EU standards.

In the EU, several countries, including France, have discontinued the wealth tax due to its unintended consequences. The implementation of the wealth tax in these regions resulted in the expatriation of wealth, which did not contribute to the domestic economy as intended. Historical precedents, such as those observed in the 1970s and in various EU countries, demonstrate that excessive taxation of income or wealth can have counterproductive effects. Currently, the EU is experiencing a shortfall in private capital. This deficiency is hindering the region's ability to emulate the successful model of the US in several key areas. These include the development of innovative technologies, the nurturing of emerging startups, and the investment in vital sectors such as Artificial Intelligence, military advancements, or even green technology.

In the US, a form of wealth taxation is already in place through the property tax levied on real estate. The US also imposes a capital gains tax, which would overlap with a concurrent wealth tax, as explained below. In contrast, Switzerland does not impose a capital gains tax on stock investments, opting only for a wealth tax.

Alternative tax on wealth: The capital gains tax

In the US, the capital gains tax exists to rein in the infinite increase in asset valuations, primarily benefiting the wealthiest individuals. This tax is imposed on the profit realized from the sale of assets, which is determined by comparing the sale price with the original purchase price. The application of capital gains tax at the exact moment of asset sale ensures a clear and unambiguous determination of the taxable amount, offering a more straightforward approach compared to the complex nature of a wealth tax.

Effective from 2020, the US federal tax regime imposes a 37% capital gains tax on short-term investments, categorized as assets held for a duration of less than one year. This federal rate is further augmented by state-level taxes, with California imposing taxes as high as 13.3%. However, this short-term rate is infrequently paid by wealthy individuals. This is because such individuals commonly engage in short-term trading through hedge funds based in tax havens. These hedge funds are not subject to taxation, provided the assets are continuously traded and remain within the funds.

As of 2024, the federal tax rate on long-term holdings has been reduced to 20%. There are several reasons put forward to justify this lower rate. First, the earnings of shareholders have already been subjected to corporate taxes. Second, the tax structure needs to take into account the potential losses investors face due to the high failure rates of startups. Third, studies suggest that raising capital gains tax rates has led to decreased revenue for the IRS. This reduction is attributed to the tendency of individuals to avoid taxation by keeping their assets, possibly within foreign hedge funds, while resorting to borrowing against these holdings for personal expenditures until a future reduction in tax rates. Finally, taxing capital gain tends to produce cyclical revenue that fluctuates with Wall Street's business cycles. This volatility makes it challenging to reliably forecast public spending.

The tax rates currently in place are the focus of extensive debates, which fall beyond the scope of this book. Nonetheless, it is noteworthy to mention that these forms of taxation present a more feasible approach to asset taxation when compared to the challenges associated with implementing a wealth tax.

Taxing unrealized capital gains has been proposed as a measure aimed at high-net-worth individuals who rarely sell their stocks and therefore pay little in capital gains. Only a few thousand wealthy individuals would be targeted by this proposal. They would sell some shares to obtain the cash to pay the tax, but not enough to trigger the kind of unrealistic hot-potato dynamic described with a wealth tax.

The opponents of such taxation blocked it in Congress for reasons similar to the rejection of a wealth tax. They insist that such a tax would be counterproductive:

• Redirection of Investment Funds: Opponents argue that this tax would divert money away from private investments, which they contend are usually managed more efficiently than government projects. If those funds shift to government control, the economy could slow down—and in the long run, tax revenue might even shrink instead of increase.

• Disproportionate Impact on Successful Entrepreneurs: The structure of this tax places a burden on highly successful business owners. As the value of their assets increases, so does their tax liability. This could force prominent entrepreneurs, like Elon Musk, to scale back on innovative projects, and philanthropists, like Bill Gates, to curtail their charitable activities, in favor of meeting tax obligations—a scenario perceived as favoring bureaucracy.

• Competitive Disadvantage for Domestic Investors: Finally, critics argue that such a tax is un-American in spirit, as it would place American investors at a relative disadvantage compared to foreign investors who would be exempt from this tax.

The inescapable tax on wealth: The estate tax

An alternative method for taxing wealth is through estate and gift taxes, which levy taxes at the point of inheritance. Beneficiaries can opt to liquidate assets and pay the tax due through an installment plan spanning ten years, a provision permitted by the IRS. This strategy offers a more manageable payment system compared to a recurring wealth tax. It is important to note that the estate tax is closely linked with the gift tax. This linkage is designed to prevent individuals from circumventing the estate tax by transferring their wealth as gifts during their lifetime.

In the US, the federal law imposes a tax of up to 40% on inheritances or gifts exceeding $14 million. Additionally, 13 states levy their own estate tax. This $14 million federal exemption doesn't dent the collection of the estate tax on the super-rich, as their fortunes often measure in the billions, making this exemption a negligible portion of their total wealth.

The exemption is designed to protect small businesses, such as corporations and farms, facilitating their retention within the same family across generations. It serves as an incentive for small business owners, encouraging them to pursue long-term investments. It assures them that they can bequeath their entire business to their heirs without the encumbrance of estate tax. This promotes the continuity and stability of family-owned enterprises.

An alternative approach to taxing the wealthy could involve implementing taxes on luxury consumption. This method targets conspicuous expenditure rather than imposing a general wealth tax, which could potentially hinder investment, slow economic growth, and adversely affect low-income workers.

This concept was put into practice in the US in 1991, with the introduction of a 10% surcharge tax on high-end items such as yachts, private jets, jewelry, and other luxury goods. However, this tax was short-lived; just two years after its implementation, it was repealed following lobbying efforts, particularly from the luxury yacht industry, which pointed to job losses as a consequence of the tax.

In a free-market economy, not all forms of taxation can be effectively integrated. It is crucial to establish a fiscal equilibrium that stimulates economic growth and job creation while optimizing long-term tax revenue.

No miracle in plundering the rich

The idea that taxing the wealthy alone can solve climate change, low wages and inequality is a misconception. This stems from the fact that the affluent do not consume all the goods themselves; rather, they own the means of production, such as machinery and corporations. These assets are not readily convertible into liquid cash instantaneously; they represent long-term investments and are integral to the production process. Therefore, expecting immediate financial gains from their liquidation just doesn't make any sense.

This doesn't mean that a wealth tax should be dismissed. A measured approach to wealth taxation, akin to the model implemented in Switzerland, can be justified to curb the potential for undue political influence by the ultra-wealthy. However, implementing such a tax might necessitate adjustments to the current tax framework, which could include reconsidering or eliminating the capital gains tax.

On the other hand, a gigantic wealth tax will never fund the extensive creation of well-paying jobs through large-scale public works for building hospitals, roads, schools, or a green transition to fix climate change.

The only sea change that could be enacted is a confiscation of wealth, such as outright expropriation in a manner akin to historical communist regimes, or an annual 10% wealth tax leading to complete nationalization over a decade. This approach didn't revitalize the USSR or Maoist China. In many instances, it only transferred the wealth from private individuals to totalitarian masters.

The belief that the rich are only rich at the expense of the poor is simplistic. If this were the case, communist-style redistribution would have resolved such inequities. On the contrary, communist administrations of the past have significantly under-performed the free market of industrial minds and venture capitalists. Monopolistic management by apparatchiks may have kept prices low, but with long lines at the shops.

No, the Government Cannot Force Corporations to Fix It All

Shouldn't the government order corporations to clean up the planet?

There is a growing call for stringent regulations on corporations to fix it all. It already happened with the Clean Air Act that reduced pollution since the 1970s. It must happen again despite the lobbying of greedy corporations against regulations. The public must mobilize to support political leaders who are committed to enacting stringent regulations on corporations to achieve a decarbonized economy.

This program could gradually intensify these regulations. The plan would increase energy-efficiency standards to decarbonize power plants and adapt corporate machinery to use clean electricity. The strategy should also give sufficient time for the mass market to adapt and redesign products to operate on electricity, thereby mitigating potential price spikes. Ultimately, such stringent regulatory measures could accelerate the transition to environmental sustainability.

Activists advocate for strong regulation of corporations, which are often perceived as making excessive profits. They argue that such regulation is necessary to enforce stringent environmental standards, urging a shift to put the "planet over profit."

Not so fast. The majority of the selling price goes to gross wages for employees and payments to suppliers. Both workers and suppliers inevitably pass their tax burdens onto consumers through the pricing of their products and services. Of what remains, the lion's share is allocated to government taxes, which fund various expenditures—not always sound investments and sometimes even pork-barrel projects. This amount cover a wide range of taxes, from sales taxes benefiting local governments to income taxes contributing to federal revenue, as well as taxes on the workers employed by corporations. Altogether, the government's share is nearing 30% of the selling price, as measured by the ""tax-to-GDP ratio."

For their part, US corporations earn an average profit margin of only 8% per sale, according to data on 7,000 firms in the NYU Stern database (source: AEI.org).

This suggests that governments, rather than corporations, may be the primary beneficiaries in the economy, implying that the "planet over profit" mantra should perhaps be directed at addressing the role of governments as well.

Energy-efficiency: A few simple regulations

Various governments have implemented regulatory measures aimed at reducing the environmental impact of economic activities. These regulations have been designed to target areas that do not necessitate extensive bureaucratic oversight for enforcement and have minimal impact on economic growth and job creation. This approach allows consumers to transition to energy-efficient alternatives within moderate budgetary constraints.

In the US, regulatory measures introduced in 2015 include:

• Gas mileage: The US target is around 32 mpg, in comparison the EU target is over 45 mpg (based on CAFE measurements).

• Coal-burning plants: The Environmental Protection Agency (EPA) introduced regulations aimed at phasing out the oldest coal-burning power plants. These plants are to be replaced with facilities powered by natural gas, which has become cheaper due to advancements in hydraulic fracturing (fracking) techniques.

• Energy-efficiency in building codes: Regulations have been established to enhance energy efficiency in new building constructions. These include standards for improved insulation and the installation of movement detector light switches.

In the US, the follow-up of these regulations depends on the political majority in Congress. The 2015 regulations stemming from the Obama administration were a series of presidential directives that were not subjected to a congressional vote. These directives were subsequently challenged in court and partially rolled back by the Trump administration, which deemed them detrimental to jobs in sectors such as automobile manufacturing and coal mining. Once again, under President Biden's administration, a revised set of fuel economy standards was reimplemented, still without a vote in Congress.

Tightening the screw too fast: Bankruptcies guaranteed

Congress is hesitant to go faster, acknowledging the challenges faced by corporations, particularly smaller ones, in adapting to green initiatives. Large corporations might have the capacity to self-fund and efficiently transition to green practices. However, smaller corporations often lack the necessary financial resources for such a transition.

The abrupt imposition of stringent energy standards requiring corporations to decarbonize could create serious difficulties, especially for smaller firms. Such a forced transition would demand new processes, workforce retraining, revised supply chains, and even redesigned product lines. These added costs would likely drive companies to raise their prices—particularly smaller businesses with limited economies of scale compared to larger competitors. Failure to do so could result in chronic unprofitability, loan denials, insolvency, and ultimately bankruptcy, since expenses such as wages, taxes, and interest charges cannot be concealed in accounting.

This worst-case scenario for small businesses could reduce national output, as large corporations would face less competition, potentially weakening innovation, efficiency, and long-term growth. Larger firms may also be less inclined to fill the gap left by bankrupt small businesses, especially in the short term. The result could be rising unemployment, economic disruption, and a slowdown in overall economic activity.

Costs passed onto consumers?

The acceleration of energy-efficiency timelines could impose a burden on both large and small corporations. These companies might face losses due to the sudden obsolescence of machinery used in the production of non-compliant, environmentally unfriendly products. This machinery, once central to their operations, could become functionally useless almost overnight. Furthermore, corporations would find themselves in a competitive market for limited resources. The demand for green energy solutions and environmentally friendly equipment, such as electric ovens or battery-powered vehicles, is likely to exceed supply. Given the insufficient time for the mass market to adjust and scale up production, these green alternatives could be prohibitively expensive.

It would leave few choices for corporations to stay afloat. In most instances, corporations would have to raise their sale prices to cover the green conversion costs. Corporations must always include all their costs, wages, taxes, and interest charge in their selling prices. They must do so, as they can't remain unprofitable for long, or face loan rejections, insolvency, and ultimately bankruptcy.

The high green prices would ultimately burden final consumers. These higher costs might be paid at the expense of other household budgets, such as clothing or entertainment. This reallocation of spending could create ripple effects in other sectors, reducing output and shedding jobs. Finally, those at the lower end of the economic spectrum may be disproportionately affected, as they typically spend a larger share of their income on energy-related expenses.

Communist movements often highlight Cuba's low carbon footprint and present it as a viable model for broader implementation.

Actually, it is a misconception to attribute Cuba's low carbon footprint to its communist model. This outcome resulted more from geopolitical circumstances than from a deliberate environmental strategy. Key factors included the US embargo, which hindered Cuba's ability to import oil, the end of subsidized oil shipments from the Soviet Union in the early 1990s, and the Cuban economy's inability to afford costly oil imports even from friendly nations.

In the end, Cuba's lower emissions were not a proactive achievement of the regime but rather a forced adaptation to external economic pressures. The country instead illustrates what a frugal lifestyle and limited personal freedom might look like under a government imposing strict control to maintain a low carbon footprint.

Corporations cannot fix the climate alone

The transition of corporations to fully sustainable processes and outputs is contingent on consumer participation. Consumers cannot simply splurge on green electricity or stockpile batteries, given constraints such as scarce metals and necessary environmental regulations. They must also recognize their own role in this transition, rather than shifting all responsibility to others. Household consumption accounts for roughly 70% of US GDP, with the remaining 30% split between corporate investment and government expenditure. This highlights the outsized impact of consumer behavior on both the economy and environmental sustainability.

Unchecked consumption would force companies to raise prices—a necessary response to the rising costs of the green transition, particularly in the face of raw material shortages and production delays. A successful transition therefore requires collaboration across all sectors of the economy: corporations must innovate and deliver better products, while consumers must make more conscientious purchasing decisions. Only through this shared effort can a sustainable balance be achieved between environmental responsibility and economic viability.

No, Frugality Is Not the Remedy

Frugality through household quotas?

Adopting a frugal lifestyle can contribute to reducing carbon emissions. This involves limiting consumption as much as possible, even before prioritizing the purchase of green products. For example, one might grow vegetables in the garden before going to the grocery store. Travel would rely primarily on bicycles, with air travel kept to a minimum.

To reinforce this lifestyle, consumption quotas for each household could be introduced. This system is not novel; it mirrors existing models such as tiered pricing in utilities, where electricity and water costs escalate once consumption exceeds a predetermined baseline. Similarly, the insurance industry employs a bonus-malus system, adjusting premiums based on an individual's claim history. Historical precedents include the implementation of rationing during wartime, regulating the distribution of essentials like grain, sugar, and fuel. However, it is notable that in peacetime, quotas often apply in the opposite direction with discounts on bulk purchasing.

The proposed system should involve devising and gradually integrating new quotas across various economic sectors. This approach would ensure equitable pricing for low-income households up to a baseline quantity, while imposing higher costs on wealthier households for excessive consumption. Proponents argue that this method could effectively address environmental challenges.

A monastic, self-sufficient lifestyle centered on small-scale farming and minimal consumption has faced criticism for creating a parasitic dynamic rather than exemplifying heroic sustainability. Historical precedents, such as the back-to-the-land movement of the 20th century, illustrate how such lifestyles can depend heavily on public services, including healthcare and infrastructure, funded by the broader taxpayer base engaged in the traditional economy.

Previous attempts at such reforms have often led to reduced crop yields and increased risk of food scarcity, particularly affecting urban populations. Contributing factors include suboptimal land use, the limited effectiveness of homemade fertilizers, reliance on outdated agricultural methods, and the inability to benefit from economies of scale. These deficiencies have frequently necessitated a reversal of these policies.

Energy quotas: Circumvented by the rich

Enforcement of a frugality-oriented quota system may present challenges in reaching affluent individuals, largely because of their ample resources and potential to devise methods to bypass such restrictions. In practice, the rich would adapt to a quota system with relative ease, requiring only minor modifications in their expenditure habits. Their options might include:

- Paying the Tiered Charges: Wealthy individuals can easily afford higher-tier electricity or natural gas rates for exceeding the baseline quota, a policy that applies to both affluent and less affluent consumers equally.

• Investing in Alternative Energy: Affluent individuals might invest in green solutions to circumvent energy quotas. They have the financial capacity to rapidly transition to carbon-neutral living and reduce their reliance on fossil fuels. This can involve investments in home insulation, rooftop solar panels, ground-source heat pumps, or electric vehicles. By doing so, they can effectively bypass restrictions on electricity, natural gas, or gasoline consumption. However, these choices can also concentrate demand for critical minerals (e.g., lithium, nickel, rare earths) and scarce installation capacity, potentially disadvantaging others.

• Exploiting Legal Loopholes: Similar to their approach with taxation, wealthy individuals might seek and exploit legal loopholes in an extended quota system with bureaucratic limits set on purchases of certain environmentally friendly products like heat pumps or solar panels.

It is important to note that only under extreme circumstances, such as in a totalitarian regime or a wartime economy, could a more rigid quota system be effectively enforced. In most current contexts, such stringent regulation is not a part of the policy discussion.

Energy quotas would burden low-income households

The imposition of stricter frugality measures may not be a viable option for all segments of the population. Particularly, the lower half of the income spectrum might strongly resist such policies. These groups often perceive such efforts as a form of "green conspicuousness" or environmental elitism. They are generally opposed to having their consumption habits dictated or judged by more affluent segments of society, highlighting a socio-economic divide in attitudes towards environmental conservation measures.

In the US, many households living paycheck to paycheck already maintain a frugal lifestyle out of necessity. Their limited financial means restrict their ability to further reduce consumption, especially when it comes to investing in energy-saving measures.

Any investment required to cope with consumption quotas would disproportionately affect low-income households, as energy costs represent a significantly higher share of their budgets compared with wealthier households. According to the US Department of Energy, low-income families spend three times more of their income on energy than other households. Contributing factors include living in under-insulated homes and using inefficient heating and cooling systems as well as outdated appliances.

Middle-class Americans would also struggle to invest in sustainable solutions, often for practical reasons. Apartment ownership can limit the ability to make environmental upgrades due to space constraints. This includes installing solar panels, heat pumps, or electric vehicle chargers, which typically require more space than apartments can provide. Moreover, eligibility criteria for energy-saving programs frequently exclude middle-income groups. For instance, the US federal Weatherization Assistance Program for Low-Income Persons disqualifies households of four earning above $53,000 per year (as of 2021).

Any rapid green initiative, such as quotas for a swift transition away from fossil fuels, poses a risk of overwhelming the financial stability of the low to middle-income classes. Imposing these quotas or restrictions on energy consumption based on current usage levels could unfairly strain the budgets of the less affluent half of the country. Such measures must consider the economic disparities and strive for equitable solutions that do not unduly burden those with limited financial resources.

Energy efficiency is essential in the shift towards sustainable energy practices, particularly given the slow scaling up of green energy production. Recognizing this, the IEA has identified energy efficiency as a key priority. Households could play a significant role in reducing energy demand. This transition requires not only holding corporations accountable but also implementing measures by individuals, such as investing in electric vehicles or improving home insulation. However, involving middle-class households remains a challenge.

Strict quotas could disrupt demand and employment

The swift enforcement of austerity measures could reduce the consumption of mainstream products. This shift might occur if environmentally friendly alternatives are not yet able to scale production to meet new demand. Such a rapid change could slow economic growth, increase unemployment, and exacerbate income inequality.

A strategy of strict quotas can be as detrimental as imposing heavy taxes and rigorous regulations. This assertion aligns with the negative impact caused by government intervention, in terms of unemployment and widening income disparities. Workers in lower-income brackets might suffer disproportionately, facing reductions in wages or even job losses, particularly in sectors affected by the green transition, such as coal mining, oil extraction, and cement manufacturing. Any plan for transition must avoid economic hardship, even if motivated by the noble goal of combating climate change.

Entrenched inequalities make implementing quotas easier said than done and often render such measures politically untenable. Public opinion polls show that concerns about inequality often rank above combating climate change in importance. Low-income households, already grappling with underemployment and persistent disparities, may view harsh environmental measures as provocative. This sentiment can influence electoral outcomes, favoring candidates who oppose environmental regulations perceived as worsening economic inequality —especially when such disparities have endured for decades.

Accordingly, it is imperative to incorporate compensatory measures to ensure a transition that does not worsen inequalities. This approach must navigate the complexities of economic and environmental objectives. This strategy will be discussed in the forthcoming sections.

Some people believe that the excessive consumption of fossil fuels is directly correlated with overpopulation, attributed to high birth rates. Observing families with numerous children (as in the picture), they perceive this demographic trend as a risk to global sustainability. As a consequence, they advocate for the implementation of birth rate control measures.

Historically, high child mortality rates, due to the lack of hygiene and medical care, necessitated larger families, as many children did not survive into adulthood.

However, over recent decades, there has been a global decline in birth rates, largely influenced by advancements in child healthcare and the adoption of family planning practices. Contrary to the notion of a "child-population bomb," the global number of births is declining.

The primary factor driving population growth today is increased longevity, a result of improved healthcare, consistent food availability, and access to clean water. According to statisticians like Hans Rosling, this trend towards an aging population is expected to be the main cause of population increase throughout the 21st century. Currently, approximately 1 billion people are aged over 60, with projections indicating this number will double by 2050. Meanwhile, birth rates are declining globally, except in Africa, contributing minimally to overall population growth.

Frugality is not exactly the goal

Adopting frugal habits can help mitigate global warming, but only to a limited extent. It no longer suffices to simply reduce fossil fuel use and limit CO_2 emissions, given the already high concentration of CO_2 in the atmosphere. The imperative is to achieve full carbon neutrality, going beyond mere reductions in consumption. It may even be necessary to develop innovative technologies to remove CO_2 from the atmosphere, even if global net-zero GHG emissions are reached within this century.

Beyond reasonable frugality measures, it is also critical to continue powering essential public services—such as healthcare and national defense—while simultaneously developing clean alternative power plants, which are still in their early stages.

The path forward requires vigorous effort, not passive adherence to frugality quotas, but active investment in and consumption of green products. This approach is vital for fostering the development of clean technologies and building a market for environmentally friendly goods, which, in turn, can pave the way for affordable clean energy solutions accessible to both developed and developing nations.

Endless economic growth is not absurd

Organizations like Greenpeace, the Club of Rome, and individuals such as Greta Thunberg have argued that perpetual economic growth is unsustainable, given the finite nature of physical resources.

This perspective has been criticized as a misunderstanding of economic fundamentals. Critics contend that the economy is more than the consumption of material goods, and that growth encompasses not only tangible production but also intangible services—such as entertainment and healthcare—which offer a pathway to growth with minimal waste. They further contend that growth in sectors tied to environmental sustainability—such as clean energy initiatives and recycling programs—constitutes genuine economic expansion. They conclude that imposing restrictions on GDP growth is not only unnecessary but may also hinder efforts to achieve sustainability targets.

Finally, economic growth remains the most effective tool for reducing unemployment. Advocates of this view maintain that expansion should continue, particularly through the development of green technologies, recycling programs, carbon-neutral energy production, and initiatives to remediate past environmental damage.

Not less but more for the green transition

Rich countries have a responsibility to develop and disseminate innovative technologies that aim not only to reduce consumption but also to foster a sustainable future. This imperative is underscored by international agreements such as COP21, which advocate for the transfer of green technologies and financial compensation to developing countries in the name of past pollution by the rich countries.

Western green tech must progress with the hard work of many. National research and corporate investments must produce affordable green products that can compete with, and ultimately surpass, fossil fuels worldwide. This includes pioneering new recycling methods and carbon sequestration services that could contribute to a reduction in atmospheric CO_2 levels.

Similarly, innovations in food production technologies are essential for rich and poor countries alike. This encompasses the integration of biotechnology, efficient water management, and the utilization of greenhouse agriculture to enhance food security for a growing global population in a warming planet.

The development of other technologies must also continue unabated, supporting the myriad needs of a functioning society. It is not feasible to halt progress in sectors deeply intertwined with the current energy-intensive economy, including the production of plastics, the technological exchanges by road, and electricity powering research laboratories. Finally, technology must always supply high-tech weapons for defending the nation from invaders, who will not stop improving their military.

In summary, the pursuit of technological innovation is indispensable for achieving a sustainable, secure, and prosperous future. It is imperative that wealthy nations lead these efforts, facilitating a transition that aligns with global environmental objectives while ensuring the continued advancement and well-being of society at large.

Part 3

GOVERNMENTS NUDGING

TIMIDLY THE ECONOMY

The UN, along with the IPCC and annual COP conferences, continues to emphasize that climate change is a serious global threat and that countries must share the responsibility of reducing carbon emissions. However, the incremental approach they have promoted has yielded limited results—mainly because climate change is more of an economic challenge than a purely political one.

These top-down, incremental regulations have so far failed to inspire broad support, even though they are still presented as the only viable path. The issue remains largely unresolved, and coverage of the issue is often so discouraging that many policymakers set it aside—except during the yearly COP meetings. While climate change may have faded from daily headlines, it is certain to return as global temperatures continue to rise.

COP21 and the Push for Market Participation

COP21 is not an economic policy per se

During the COP21, participating nations committed to reducing their greenhouse gas emissions as part of a global effort to mitigate climate change.

The table below outlines the major greenhouse gas emitters, excluding emissions from land-use change and forestry, along with their pledges made in 2015:

Country	Share of GHG emissions as of 2022 (source: EU Commission "Edgar database" = "*")	GHG (in CO_2 eq) metric tons per capita (*)	Pledge
China	29.2%	10.9	Peak emission by 2030 and reduce emissions later.
USA	11.2%	17.9	26% reduction by 2025 compared to 2005
EU-27	6.7%	8.1	40% reduction by 2030 compared to 1990 levels
India	7.3%	2.8	33% reduction by 2030, compared to 2005 levels
Russia	4.8%	18	25% reduction by 2030 compared to 1990 levels
Japan	2.2%	9.4	26% reduction by 2030 compared to 2013 levels
Others	38.6%	Most below 6	Various reduction pledges

COP21 should not be misconstrued as an economic policy. The agreement did not provide a blueprint for reconciling the apparent contradiction between economic growth and the costly measures needed to combat global warming. It leaves the onus on each country to implement its own economic system to fulfill its commitments while navigating the socio-economic impacts of regulations aimed at mitigating climate change.

The agreement reached at COP21 can be characterized as a foundational yet minimalistic accord, born out of the necessity to act in the absence of a compelling alternative. Acknowledging that initiating action, however incremental, is preferable to inaction, the agreement marks a first step with unsure economic ramifications.

Following the COP21 summit, subsequent COP's have noted a lack of significant progress.

Developing nations have expressed a desire for compensation for adhering to their COP21 commitments, arguing that industrialized nations are responsible for past CO_2 emissions accumulated in the atmosphere. These developing nations seek financial and technological support to avoid utilizing their coal reserves—a path previously taken by wealthier nations in the last century. In this sense, GHG emissions continue to rise, particularly in countries like India and China, which have been slow to implement emission reduction measures.

The need for more ambitious commitments beyond those made at COP21 is evident. There is hope that future negotiations will be supported by anticipated reductions in the costs of alternative energy sources and energy-efficient technologies, facilitating a smoother transition away from fossil fuels. Although relying on the affordability of green technologies may not be the most prudent approach, it currently represents the primary strategy of the international community in the absence of alternative solutions.

A global market without carbon border adjustments

COP21 was designed to catalyze global action and prevent a standoff, where nations were reluctant to make unilateral moves in reducing GHG emissions due to economic and geopolitical concerns. The hesitation stemmed from a reluctance to impose stringent GHG reduction measures that might adversely affect the national economy, particularly if such efforts were not reciprocated globally, potentially leaving any proactive country at a competitive disadvantage.

The fear of undermining national competitiveness was palpable. Domestic industries facing stringent carbon regulations could be compelled to divert investments toward low-carbon technologies, incurring costs not borne by their international counterparts. This discrepancy could disadvantage domestic products both abroad and at home, potentially worsening national employment.

Moreover, concerns extended to national security, with countries wary of compromising their defense capabilities, which are often seen as dependent on economic strength. For instance, the US expressed reservations about jeopardizing its role in maintaining international stability, prioritizing it over stringent GHG emission reductions that could potentially empower less democratic regimes.

The envisioned solution is a coordinated global effort towards decarbonization, stimulating a worldwide market demand that benefits from economies of scale, thereby lowering production costs and fostering competitive pricing for low-carbon products. Such an approach would circumvent the need for "carbon border adjustments" or tariffs intended to level the playing field for countries making unilateral efforts to combat climate change. The introduction of these adjustments could complicate global trade with a web of treaties, regulations, and tariffs, potentially weakening international trade dynamics and stifling competition.

The United Nations (symbolized by its flag in the picture) does not function as a global government with the authority to enforce legally binding quotas to combat global warming. Its influence is limited, as member states have conferred minimal powers upon it, preferring instead to focus on their national interests, including the advancement of their military capabilities.

The prospect of enhancing the authority of a supranational entity like the UN is fraught with challenges. A pertinent illustration of these difficulties is the European endeavor for economic and political integration. Despite ambitions for unity, European nations have been reluctant to cede significant political authority or fiscal resources to the European Union's headquarters in Brussels, which presently oversees a mere 1% of Europe's GDP. Furthermore, European governments must reach unanimous agreement to collaborate on matters, a process that often results in impasse.

Given these challenges within Europe, the idea of establishing a worldwide governance capable of managing diverse regions such as the Western World, the Middle East, the Far East, and the Southern Hemisphere appears highly improbable. This reality suggests that a shift towards such global governance, particularly to address the pressing issue of global warming, is unlikely to materialize in the foreseeable future.

Pressuring governments to act

The COP21 agreement, alongside advocacy efforts from environmental activists, aims to persuade the public of the imminent implementation of more environmentally friendly regulations. Each government that ratified the COP21 agreement has committed to meeting specific targets for reducing GHG emissions. This commitment is expected to catalyze national legislative action facilitating an ecological transition. Measures could include establishing fuel efficiency standards, providing subsidies for sustainable practices, implementing carbon-pricing mechanisms, and streamlining the permit processes for mining essential metals. Signatory countries possess the autonomy to tailor their approach, utilizing a combination of regulatory, taxation, and subsidy tools to either voluntarily or mandatorily advance towards a net-zero economy.

The COP21 agreement envisions a spectacular industrial shift towards clean energy. This call for an industrial transformation is not without historical precedent. Notably, some analysts draw parallels between the current push for renewable energy and the extensive retooling of industries for armament production during World War II. In that era, a unified effort by unions, corporations, and political leaders supported the war effort, with automobile production shifting to tank manufacturing. The surge of patriotism following the attack on Pearl Harbor enabled the implementation of rationing, corporations sacrificing profits for national interests, and the suppression of public dissent.

Achieving a similar mobilization for climate action today presents a multifaceted set of challenges:

• Accepting economic inequality, where the burden of transition may disproportionately fall on lower-income individuals expected to accept soldier pay without complaint;

• Guaranteeing the provision of green technology to developing countries, while simultaneously reducing emissions domestically;

• Sustaining these efforts over a few decades, until a full carbon-neutral economy.

The hierarchical model of compliance and leadership that was effective during World War II might not seamlessly apply in today's scenario. Contemporary challenges, particularly the pervasive skepticism towards the affluent elite, may pose significant obstacles to achieving a consensus and coordinated action on climate change.

Convincing markets of an inevitable shift

In light of impending regulatory changes, the private sector is expected to act. Investors, corporations, and consumers alike should accelerate the shift away from fossil-fuel dependence.

Investors can drive the shift towards sustainability by funding green initiatives and responding to the growing consumer demand for eco-friendly products. Through divestment, they can exert pressure on companies to adopt sustainable practices. The adoption of Environmental, Social, and Governance (ESG) criteria aims to standardize green benchmarks, distinguishing genuine sustainability efforts from "greenwashing," which involves misleading stakeholders about the environmental benefits of a product or service.

Corporations are tasked with the challenge of innovating and producing cost-effective carbon-neutral technologies. This involves enhancing technological efficiencies, establishing sustainable supply chains, and achieving economies of scale to reduce the cost of renewable energy solutions and energy-efficient products.

Following the initial phase of exploration and adaptation, it is hoped that market dynamics will propel rapid growth. A virtuous cycle of falling prices, rising sales, and expanded production is expected to drive costs down further, potentially triggering exponential market expansion.

Some remain optimistic about this scenario in the near term, while others adopt a more cautious outlook on the pace of change.

The Government's Carrot: Subsidies

Subsidies to attract participants

In the pursuit of COP21 objectives, the governments of the US and the EU find it impractical to impose rapid energy efficiency measures or an outright prohibition of fossil fuels. Such approaches, characterized by their reliance on scarce mineral resources, high costs, and potential for job destruction, could create opportunities for radical political candidates who prioritize job creation and retreat from environmental considerations.

Instead, governments tend to adopt a moderate approach aimed at mitigating economic hardships. A prevalent strategy involves subsidy programs to incentivize the production and consumption of clean electricity and other environmentally sustainable goods. These products often face difficulties competing with fossil fuel-driven alternatives on a cost basis. These subsidies are typically provided through checks, tax breaks, or tax credits, encouraging the adoption of clean energy and green products while alleviating economic burdens.

While the government may provide tax breaks and subsidies, these financial incentives often fall short of fully offsetting the tax burden embedded in the selling price of green products. For example, solar panels face significant taxation at various stages of their production and use. This includes income taxes on the earnings of workers involved in manufacturing and installation, which ultimately raise the final price. Moreover, individuals must generally purchase solar panels with post-tax income unless specific tax credits are provided.

On the other hand, gasoline in the US is subject to relatively low taxation. Moreover, the petroleum industry, being less labor-intensive than the installation of solar panels or wind turbines, may contribute less to income tax revenues generated from the workforce.

Under the current tax framework, individuals pursuing a transition from fossil fuels to renewable energy sources may find themselves subjected to taxes, while petroleum-based energy enjoys a more lenient tax regime. This situation not only makes the shift toward eco-friendly practices less financially attractive but also creates an unfair competitive advantage for the lower-taxed petroleum industry.

Only about nurturing green products

Subsidies are designed to promote the production and adoption of emerging green technologies, such as solar panels, wind turbines, electric vehicles, and batteries, within the marketplace through a two-fold approach. Initially, they aim to enable green products to compete effectively with fossil-fuel-based counterparts and gain market traction. Subsequently, the goal is to scale up production to lower the unit costs of green products through economies of scale.

To date, prices have not dropped sufficiently to catalyze widespread market adoption and displace fossil-fuel-based products, with the exception of niche markets catering to environmentally conscious consumers (e.g., Tesla vehicles or residential solar panels) or specific regions well-suited for green energy (e.g., wind farms in Oklahoma).

The question remains whether prices will continue to decline, prompting a shift from polluting products to cheaper, cleaner alternatives. Extending subsidy programs may be necessary beyond the initial nurturing phase to support this transition.

Shouldn't the widely discussed subsidies extended to oil and coal corporations be eliminated to create a more level playing field for green products? In reality, these so-called "**fossil fuel subsidies**" are not direct financial gifts from the government to the oil and coal industries aimed at artificially lowering the price of fossil fuels. Instead, they encompass a range of measures that may raise concerns. For instance, initiatives like funding road construction in Alaska or providing assistance to airports impacted by the Covid crisis have been labeled as "subsidies to fossil fuels." Another example is the estimation by the International Monetary Fund (IMF) that places these "subsidies" at approximately 6.5% of GDP. This figure includes certain tax incentives but primarily encompasses exemptions granted to the oil and coal sectors to address the environmental consequences of fossil fuel consumption, which are borne by consumers. Many argue that these studies on subsidies are flawed and are leveraged to justify placing the responsibility for combating global warming on the oil and coal industry.

What could be the consequences if this proposal to reduce subsidies were implemented? In one scenario, oil and coal corporations might pass on the costs of the subsidy reduction to consumers. This would result in higher fossil fuel prices and trigger an economic "oil shock," disproportionately affecting the most vulnerable segments of society, as is often the case during crises.

Alternatively, if oil and coal companies were to absorb the costs of airport bailouts, pollution mitigation efforts, and other expenses without increasing product prices, they might scale back their investments, while countries like Saudi Arabia increase their oil sales.

In the event of aggressive "subsidy defunding," oil and coal corporations could go bankrupt, disrupting gasoline deliveries, breaking supply chains, and ultimately affecting people's access to food and electricity.

It is essential to recognize that the oversimplified notion of "subsidy defunding" can be demagogic and does not offer a solution to the challenges associated with transitioning away from fossil fuels.

Extending subsidies: Cost concerns

In the initial stages, subsidy programs were designed to have a negligible impact on the government's budget, particularly when the green market was in its nascent phase. During this period, solar panels or wind turbines were produced in limited quantities and involved subsidy programs of modest scale.

In the present phase of a potential full-scale green transition, expanding subsidy programs is fiscally challenging. Subsidies must remain high to make green products competitive, and they would quickly strain the Treasury as they continue to cover the cost difference between green products and fossil fuels. For this reason—and because other budget priorities take precedence—subsidy programs remain limited.

Extending subsidies: Market distortion

The government is even considering phasing out subsidy programs before the economy has fully transitioned away from fossil fuels. This move is justified by the view that green products are becoming increasingly competitive and that subsidies are criticized for "distorting the market":

• Price distortion: Prolonged subsidies can distort market prices. This happens when providers rely on subsidies without making further efforts to reduce costs, since their selling price is fixed and guaranteed for an extended period. As a result, subsidy amounts in multi-year contracts—such as those for electricity from renewable sources or the production of electric vehicles—have steadily declined alongside technological progress. The ultimate goal is for these subsidies to fall to zero as green products become competitive with coal- or natural-gas-powered alternatives. At that point, market prices could decline naturally, without being tied to subsidy contracts.

• Hard to anticipate: Subsidy programs can introduce uncertainty into market expectations. A shift in the congressional majority can change the subsidies that corporations expect, complicating long-term forecasting.

• Arbitrary: Subsidies may at times seem arbitrary in how they are allocated to providers. This is because they are often tied to unpredictable budget negotiations within the legislative process, which can involve pork-barrel spending, new taxes, or deficits.

For example, the US federal subsidies on electric vehicles vary based on the capacity of the battery. Notably, these subsidies expired in 2021 for manufacturers like Chevrolet and Tesla but remained available for BMW and Chrysler, despite the latter having lower sales figures.

Another noteworthy example is a subsidy exclusively for manufacturers employing unionized workers. This decision-making process may have been influenced more by political considerations than by the genuine reduction of carbon emissions.

These instances highlight the potential for the government to overlook the merits of emerging technologies, selectively endorse certain companies over others, and inadvertently dissuade corporations from making long-term investments.

The Inflation Reduction Act (as signed into law by President Biden in the picture) presents a potential avenue for reducing greenhouse gas emissions in the US by an estimated 10% between 2023 and 2030. This would complement the expected 30% reduction in emissions from 2005 to 2030, a trend driven by the transition from coal to cheap natural gas extracted through fracking, as well as the outsourcing of the most polluting industries. These factors have already contributed to a 20% reduction in emissions from 2005 to 2020.

There are notable reservations about the complexity of the Inflation Reduction Act, a 755-page document that establishes numerous subsidy programs. These concerns stem from fears that eligibility for subsidies may be limited to corporations employing unionized workers. Moreover, the potential for companies to expand their customer base through sales of electric vehicles or solar panels to subsidized households may be constrained. Electric vehicles often require access to a private garage for charging, and solar panel installation typically excludes renters and apartment owners, who lack control over their rooftops and may feel left out.

Extending subsidies: Complex and unfair to consumers

The introduction of subsidies in Congress can introduce complications that discriminate against consumers and, at times, miss the fundamental objective of carbon reduction. These complexities are evident on the consumer side, presenting several implementation challenges:

• Bureaucratic hurdles: Subsidy programs necessitate administrative processes aimed at ensuring control and preventing fraudulent claims. Such red tape can overwhelm the poorest, as failure to complete the required paperwork or meet complex prerequisites can render the subsidy uncertain or inaccessible. This, in turn, disrupts consumers' ability to make informed price comparisons.

• Equity concerns: Subsidies can inadvertently favor affluent green-conscious households that view solar panel incentives as an added value to their properties. In contrast, renters do not have ownership of the roof, and apartment owners often share the roof, rendering them ineligible for solar panel subsidies. This disparity raises questions about fairness and equitable access to green incentives.

• Disconnect from carbon reduction objectives: Subsidies may be applied to products with similar functionalities but vastly different carbon footprints during their respective production cycles. Additionally, while subsidies can lower the prices of green appliances, they may not necessarily address the issue of overconsumption of resources, such as heating with open windows.

Paperwork for subsidies can be dissuasive. According to the President's Biden White House website: "Administrative burdens make it harder for millions of individuals, families, and small businesses to receive government benefits and services for which they may be eligible. For some individuals, families or small businesses, these burdens —costs like the "time tax" required to learn about a program, fill out paperwork, assemble required documents, and schedule visits to government offices—completely prevent access to much-needed benefits. The Office of Information and Regulatory Affairs is working to [...] reduce those burdens." This implies that one bureaucracy is attempting to fix another. A more effective approach could involve implementing tax reductions for low-income households without adding any additional bureaucracy.

The Government's Stick: Carbon Pricing

Carbon pricing: Fines for consuming fossil fuels

In advancing market-oriented strategies to meet the objectives outlined in the Paris Agreement (COP21), economists recommend replacing existing subsidies for eco-friendly products with fiscal penalties on fossil fuel consumption, known as "*carbon pricing*." These mechanisms aim to foster a more efficient, energy-saving environment by directly linking tax liabilities to carbon emissions. This approach grants consumers the autonomy to choose the most effective methods for reducing their carbon footprint.

Carbon pricing moves beyond the limitations of traditional bureaucratic controls and subsidy schemes by embracing a more flexible, market-driven policy. Economists have conceptualized two distinct models of carbon pricing, both designed to maximize adaptability and align with free-market principles.

Much like a carbon tax, European countries have long imposed high gasoline taxes, driving fuel prices to levels often twice as high as in the United States. Yet this measure has not eliminated the transport sector's carbon footprint. Rather than switching to electric vehicles or other low-emission alternatives, low-income European consumers have mostly focused on buying diesel or small cars, driving less, and cutting overall spending. This response does not achieve the impact needed to address inequality and unite the country in the fight against global warming.

Carbon pricing method 1: The carbon tax

The first proposed mechanism is the implementation of a *"carbon tax,"* which imposes a levy on coal sales by the ton and petroleum products by the gallon. The objective is to discourage the burning of these fuels, thereby supporting environmental commitments.

The carbon tax is considered a more adaptable solution than energy-efficiency regulations. It provides companies with a pragmatic pathway by allowing them to continue operations and offset their carbon emissions by paying the tax, rather than facing production bans for failing to meet strict regulatory standards. This approach gives businesses greater flexibility to transition away from fossil fuels at a manageable pace.

The avoidance of the carbon tax, by implication, necessitates a reduction in CO_2 emissions. Continuous investment in renewable energy, motivated by the desire to minimize tax liabilities, is anticipated to decrease carbon emissions more effectively than subsidies. In contrast, renewable energy systems funded by subsidies do not justify the need for new investments and continuous improvements.

Initially, the carbon tax would be selectively applied to major industrial consumers, including large corporations that utilize petroleum or electricity generated from non-renewable sources, thereby exempting small businesses and individual consumers from immediate impact. The expectation is that affected corporations would redirect their investments towards energy-efficient initiatives and renewable energy conversion, diminishing their carbon tax burden over time and fostering a transition to more sustainable practices.

Carbon pricing method 2: Cap-and-trade

The second mechanism introduces a regulatory limit on CO_2 emissions, referred to by various terms such as allowance-quota, carbon-offset, carbon-permit, or carbon-credit. This system establishes a ceiling or *"cap"* on the amount of CO_2 emissions that corporations can release into the atmosphere without incurring penalties. Initially, corporations are allocated allowance-quotas that permit them to emit a specified amount of CO_2.

Should a corporation wish to exceed its allocated emission cap, it must acquire additional allowances from other entities that have not used their full quota. This transaction occurs in a *"cap-and-trade"* market, where allowances can be bought and sold, either wholly or partially. The market enables entities in one sector to offset their CO_2 emissions by purchasing reductions achieved by other industries that can cut emissions at a lower cost.

Essentially, the cap-and-trade model represents a system of flexible penalties or tradable emission allowances. The trading component is designed to mitigate the rigidity of fixed emission quotas, which could disproportionately hinder production across different industries, over-look the variances between sectors, and escalate the overall cost of compliance. This approach aims to provide a more adaptable and economically efficient framework for reducing CO_2 emissions.

Carbon pricing and its wishful guidelines

The implementation of carbon pricing should follow a few guiding principles to minimize the economic distortions typically associated with taxation:

• Gradual implementation: The introduction of carbon pricing should be incremental, with the levy increasing over time. This gradual approach is intended to give corporations sufficient time to adjust to the new tax regime, facilitating a smoother transition toward a low-carbon economy.

• Tax neutral: The aim is to minimize economic disruption by substituting certain existing taxes with carbon pricing in a way that does not increase the overall tax burden. However, this approach still imposes new and complex regulatory requirements on businesses and tax professionals.

• Universal participation: The scope of carbon pricing should extend beyond the major CO_2 emitters to include small businesses and individuals. This inclusivity is crucial to prevent small enterprises from curtailing expansion due to emission threshold concerns—a scenario that could negatively impact job creation. Similarly, individuals should be accountable for their carbon emissions, given that domestic heating, vehicle use, food production, and the distribution of goods account for a good portion of direct energy consumption. This comprehensive approach aims to ensure that all sectors of the economy contribute to the collective effort of reducing carbon emissions.

In the context of meeting the objectives set forth by the Paris Agreement (COP21), the US has not successfully enacted carbon-pricing regulations. Legislative hesitation stems from concerns over the extensive measures required to combat global warming. Congress harbors apprehensions that stringent regulations aimed at reducing CO_2 emissions could have detrimental effects on the job market without guaranteeing environmental benefits. Therefore, there is a preference for a cautious approach to addressing climate change—one that avoids the gradual breakdown of social stability.

Congress maintains that an aggressive regulatory and taxation framework could quickly overburden the economy, reminiscent of the economic challenges faced during the 1970s. Poorly conceived regulations could complicate the business environment, disrupt investment, damage employment, and provoke pushback against their implementation.

Congress currently prefers to let technological innovation, market forces, and production scaling naturally progress, reducing the cost of clean energy to levels that are competitive with fossil fuels. This reliance on the advancement of green technologies and market solutions reflects a pragmatic stance, one that is often seen as the only viable option to address climate change. It aims to mitigate the impact on the middle class and avoid provoking political backlash.

Carbon pricing: Mind-boggling to implement

Should it surmount the initial challenge of Congressional approval, the implementation of a carbon tax or cap-and-trade system would face a subsequent obstacle: determining the appropriate penalties under this carbon-pricing framework. Theoretically, it requires authorities simply to set the rates for carbon taxes or prices for carbon-credits in alignment with CO_2 emission levels.

In practice, establishing these financial parameters is complex. It involves determining specific tax rates, emission caps, carbon credit costs, and incremental adjustments, all while navigating potential challenges:

• Underwhelming carbon pricing: If carbon pricing is set too low, either through underpriced carbon taxes or generous issuance of carbon credits, corporations might transfer the minimal costs of carbon pricing to consumers, especially during an economic downturn benefiting from low fossil fuel prices. This scenario could result in unchanged energy consumption patterns, with no incentive to transition to green energy sources.

• Overly stringent carbon pricing: If carbon pricing is implemented aggressively in a rapidly expanding economy with surging energy consumption, it could cause fossil fuel prices to soar. Corporations unable to adapt may have no choice but to pass these costs—compounded by the high price of carbon—on to consumers. This could make many goods unaffordable, hindering economic growth.

• Long-term cost uncertainty: Authorities' hesitance to adjust carbon pricing over time can obscure long-term costs. This complicates corporations' ability to plan financially for the future, potentially discouraging them from investing or expanding their workforce.

Each of these scenarios underscores the complexity of implementing carbon-pricing mechanisms, highlighting the need for careful calibration to avoid unintended economic consequences.

Carbon-pricing experiments are dragging on

The calibration of carbon pricing represents a formidable challenge in current experiments. Lenient carbon pricing policy initiatives imposed on corporations have proven inadequate in altering fossil fuel consumption patterns. European efforts involve continuous tinkering to the EU-ETS (European Union Emission Trading Scheme), a cap-and-trade market. Similarly, California's implementation of its cap-and-trade program has encountered difficulties, as have the nine northeastern states participating in the Regional Greenhouse Gas Initiative, which focuses on the power sector. Finally, Canada and other nations are still evaluating their respective cap-and-trade systems.

Corporations may either pay carbon taxes or purchase carbon credits, but the broader impact on fossil fuel consumption has been minimal. The gradual application of carbon pricing—intended to minimize economic disruption—has not accelerated the transition to renewable energy. Instead, the costs of carbon pricing are often passed on to consumers. At the same time, some industries are relocating to jurisdictions with fewer regulations, further complicating efforts to reduce emissions. Altogether, the aspiration to foster a robust green market through carbon pricing has yet to be realized.

Should gradual approaches continue to fall short, a steep adjustment in carbon pricing may become necessary. However, economists caution that drastic increases could severely impact the economy, presenting a challenging scenario for policymakers.

The oil shocks of the 1970s significantly influenced consumer behavior, although rising gas prices were not the only factor. In the US, for instance, 1979 saw an increase in sales of compact vehicles from Toyota and Datsun. During this period, American automakers were unprepared to offer similar fuel-efficient models and high-quality products capable of competing with the reliability of Japanese vehicles.

Similarly, economists face challenges in isolating the impact of gas prices on the popularity of fuel-efficient cars from other factors such as oil price fluctuations and broader market dynamics. This complexity extends to determining the optimal carbon tax rate that would influence corporate behavior without causing increased consumer prices. Given these uncertainties, attributing the inaction solely to a lack of political will may be unjust.

Carbon pricing: Blocked by voters discontent over low wages

Reluctance to implement carbon-pricing systems is largely due to a mammoth economic concern: the potential adverse impact on low-income households. These households spend a higher proportion of their income on energy, making them more vulnerable to any form of carbon pricing. Moreover, there is palpable fear among workers about potential job losses, particularly in industries such as coal mining.

This resistance among lower-income groups is exacerbated by persistent economic inequality, which has fostered a sense of exclusion from the benefits of economic growth and a strong rejection of environmental regulations that disproportionately affect them. This sentiment has fueled protests—as seen in France with the "Yellow Vest" movement—and has shaped the election of leaders opposed to climate action, such as President Trump, who has advocated dismantling carbon regulations viewed as punitive toward the lower middle class.

Environmental initiatives must therefore avoid the appearance of a punitive tax, even when presented as revenue-neutral. Instead, they should directly address inequality, steering clear of the perception of elitist policymaking that takes with one hand and gives back with the other. The challenge is to design carbon-pricing systems that reconcile the dual imperatives of environmental stewardship and social equity.

To address the challenges associated with carbon pricing, some have proposed integrating "carbon dividends" into these frameworks. Notably, the Baker-Shultz plan (as in the picture) suggests imposing a tax on the fossil fuel consumption of corporations and distributing the proceeds from this tax to the people as carbon dividends. This approach aims to mitigate the financial impact of carbon taxes on consumers and ensures that the revenue generated is specifically allocated to combat global warming, rather than being diverted to fund unrelated budget items.

This model could still pressure low-income households as corporations transition to costly green energy sources. During this period, carbon dividends are likely to decline while carbon pricing rises to support the transition. As a result, low-income groups may continue to face disproportionate financial burdens, leaving broader issues of economic inequality unresolved.

There may be calls for additional subsidies targeted at helping low-income populations offset the economic impact of declining carbon dividends. However, this low-income group would then lose any incentive to reduce its reliance on fossil fuels. Furthermore, such a compensation program would go back to square one and reintroduce the complexity of subsidy-based approaches, undermining the advantages of a market-driven carbon pricing system.

Carbon pricing finally implemented...
by geopolitics after 2020

Since 2021, an inadvertent form of carbon pricing has been effectively implemented, not as a result of successful carbon market initiatives, but due to geopolitical developments. The disruption of fossil fuel supplies on the international market, triggered by the combined impacts of the post-Covid recovery and the Ukraine War, has led to significant price increases.

In the US and particularly in the EU, the prices of oil and natural gas have soared. For instance, the cost of a barrel of crude oil escalated from around $50 in the pre-Covid era to over $100 following the onset of the Ukraine War. Simultaneously, natural gas prices have tripled in the US and quintupled in the EU. This price surge effectively mirrors the impact of a stringent carbon tax.

The public did not welcome this price rise any more than it accepted the broader inflation that began in 2021, even when both were likened to the potential effects of a carbon-pricing system. Corporations and consumers alike had to bear the burden of increased costs, even though carbon-pricing policies are typically aimed at large corporations. In response, governments felt compelled to ease the impact on the public by providing financial assistance to offset rising energy costs. These measures were driven by fears of public backlash, as seen with Brexit in the UK and the Yellow Vest protests in France.

These events tend to portray carbon pricing as an unrealistic option for the global effort to mitigate global warming. Some even argue that carbon pricing is no longer a viable solution.

US and EU emissions cut in half by 2030?

The coming years will be critical in determining whether there is a shift towards clean energy and green products, despite geopolitical concerns and potential economic slowdowns.

In the US, President Biden has set an ambitious goal for the nation to achieve a 50% reduction in economy-wide net greenhouse gas emissions by 2030, relative to 2005 levels.

Similarly, the EU has enacted the European Climate Law, which sets an intermediate target of reducing greenhouse gas emissions by at least 55% by 2030, compared to 1990 levels.

Should the US and the EU encounter delays in meeting these objectives, the question arises: what would constitute an effective Plan B? Would it become necessary to consider hazardous geoengineering techniques, or might an alternative path emerge to expedite the global green transition?

Part 4

WILL TECHNOLOGY

SAVE THE DAY?

Any plan to fight climate change will also have to face the impact of AI on jobs. AI is poised to reshape industries: research with cheap batteries for abundant green energy, faster drug discovery, manufacturing with affordable robots, transportation with driverless cars, and healthcare with improved medical diagnosis.

These advances raise a critical question: Will AI create jobs—including green jobs— or destroy them? Already, some software developers have lost work to AI, forcing them into lower-paying roles or unemployment. Robots and AI systems are increasingly replacing people in routine tasks—and may soon take on more advanced ones, such as loading a dishwasher.

New Technologies Could Boost the Green Economy

Technology-driven productivity could create green jobs

As green policies stall, many hope revolutionary technologies can bridge the gap. According to some pundits, advancements in artificial intelligence, quantum computing, biotechnology, and other emerging fields could catalyze rapid economic growth, higher wages and cheaper green products.

In economic terms, these technological innovations can enhance workforce efficiency, which directly contributes to *"productivity"*— defined as the ratio of output to input, such as revenue relative to capital investment. This metric, monitored by statistical agencies, serves as a key economic indicator. Productivity gains are tracked through corporate accounting data, economic surveys, and tax filings, and they encompass various aspects such as labor productivity, capital productivity, and material productivity. Such gains show how engineers and workers leverage new technologies to make investments in cheaper, better, and more innovative products more profitable.

Productivity gains have the potential to revitalize the economy. Lower production costs mean that essential goods, such as food, cars, and healthcare, become more affordable, leaving people with more disposable income. This additional income can be saved or spent on new products and services, stimulating demand in various sectors. Businesses, in turn, will respond by investing in innovations and offering new products and services, such as household robots, auto-mated meal-preparation systems, and much more.

Productivity gains: Boosting GDP growth and economic well-being

As productivity gains accumulate, they contribute to overall GDP growth and encourage further investments in profitable ventures. Higher profitability can even attract investments in sectors like green energy, making them more competitive than fossil fuels. This, in turn, creates quality employment opportunities, including green jobs, and improves the economic outlook for low-income workers.

Historical data suggests that when real GDP growth exceeds 3%, it can catalyze both employment growth and wage increases. This fast growing economy could also lead to green job creation, new green startups, and cheaper green energy.

On the contrary, if productivity gains are insufficient and GDP growth stagnate below 2%, automation and robotics may keep on supplanting human workers and exert downward pressure on wages—a concern highlighted in the first section—while few new ventures and hiring projects are being funded.

The average GDP growth rate exceeded 4% during the 1950s and 1960s, but fell to 3% in the 1970s and 1980s and has hovered around 2% since 2000 (see chart: source BEA). Will today's promising technologies spark a recovery in GDP growth—boosting the green job market and helping the fight against global warming—starting in 2024, despite inevitable downturns? Could this surge last longer than the dotcom boom of the 1990s, when GDP briefly surged above 4% for just a few euphoric years? This time, might technology be the transformative force that delivers lasting global prosperity?

AI could improve productivity across the board

Artificial Intelligence (AI) is considered a key solution to addressing the stagnation in productivity and modest GDP growth seen in recent decades. Similar to how personal computers and the internet boosted productivity in the past, AI has the potential to accelerate advancements. It can reduce costs in research-intensive industries, replace routine tasks previously handled by personal assistants, and enhance the profitability of investments by increasing efficiency across various sectors.

AI has the potential to enhance the productivity of highly skilled professionals across various industries, as discussed in the best-selling book *The Coming Wave* by Mustafa Suleyman. AI's capabilities span a wide range of applications, including refining text composition, automating initial drafts of software code, performing precise data analysis, and enabling robots to learn autonomously through trial and error. Its impact could be far-reaching, driving innovation in fields such as software development, pharmaceuticals, medical diagnostics, autonomous vehicles, quantum computing, biotechnology, cost-effective battery, efficient solar panels, advanced counseling and robotics software, and fraud detection in financial transactions, among others.

In the corporate sector, AI tools will primarily be developed within data centers operated by companies such as Amazon, Google, and Microsoft. AI research teams and consulting firms will use these resources to create advanced machine learning solutions for processing data, identifying patterns, and analyzing text, images, molecules, and algorithms. These AI specialists will help both large and small corporations design more cost-effective products and generate innovative new outputs.

Consumers will benefit from AI-optimized products designed to replace outdated and inefficient alternatives at lower costs. AI primarily focuses on optimizing existing processes rather than inventing entirely new products. For instance, AI could contribute to the development of more effective drugs, potentially reducing healthcare costs. It could also enhance agricultural productivity, making food more affordable, and enable cost-efficient production and transportation through robotics and autonomous vehicles. Furthermore, AI-powered services, such as affordable legal assistance, may become widely accessible, offering new opportunities for the general public.

Can AI and Technology Overcome All Obstacles?

Can AI boost economic growth quickly enough to create green jobs?

It is difficult to predict whether AI will benefit the green transition, the job markets, and wages. On the one hand, AI enthusiasts promise revolutionary changes, though their views may be overly optimistic due to vested interests. On the other hand, economists caution that future GDP growth driven by AI remains uncertain.

At present, AI does not directly generate widespread consumer demand or employment—aside from user-friendly applications like ChatGPT. This contrasts with the 1990s, when personal computers and the internet spurred job creation and mass consumer adoption. For now, AI remains primarily a corporate tool. Its short-term impact is more likely to be improved products or cost reductions in sectors such as pharmaceuticals, battery technology, and manufacturing. However, these innovations often replace existing products rather than create entirely new markets or job categories, as the internet once did.

In fact, AI is already contributing to job losses as companies use automation to streamline operations. AI tends to concentrate employment in a small number of high-skill data center jobs while displacing medium-skill roles, such as content editors and software developers. Future automation may also impact drivers, cashiers, and other roles through the adoption of autonomous vehicles and other AI-powered systems. Meanwhile, transitioning displaced workers into trades like welding or electrical work is not easy, as these roles require years of training and hands-on experience—something not easily addressed through quick retraining programs.

These trends point to a fundamental challenge: productivity gains from AI depend on consumer demand. Companies are unlikely to invest in more efficient or lower-cost products if consumers lack the income to buy them. If wages fall faster than prices—or if job insecurity undermines consumer confidence—spending may stagnate. Unlike the Industrial Revolution, which addressed widespread demand from a growing middle class, today's AI-driven innovations—such as cancer treatments, service robots, or green batteries—often target niche markets, including retirees or affluent households upgrading to eco-friendly technologies.

So far, economists see little evidence that AI is significantly boosting overall productivity. Many warn that while AI may improve efficiency, the benefits are not widely shared. Instead, they often flow to a small number of individuals and corporations, while many workers face job insecurity and declining household incomes.

In the long term, AI holds significant potential, though its development is likely to be uneven. Yet many workers cannot afford to wait indefinitely for wage growth. At the same time, broader challenges—such as geopolitical tensions and climate change, which are often interconnected—may disrupt the global economy before AI-driven solutions can take full effect.

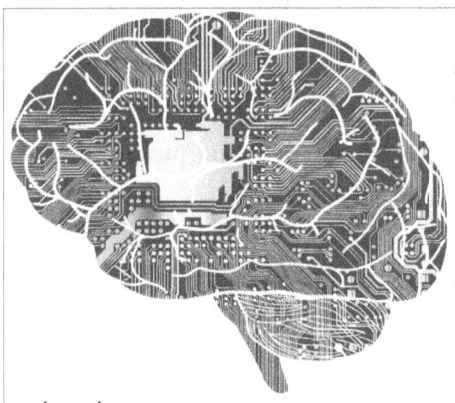

Will AGI (Artificial General Intelligence) replace worker and employee with smart robots?

Currently, no algorithms exist that can achieve the goal of human-like intelligence. AGI remains more of an aspirational concept promoted by startups seeking investment rather than an imminent reality. Despite advancements in AI, its capabilities are fundamentally limited to processing and learning from existing human-generated data without true independent reasoning or creativity.

This limitation implies that AI, as it stands today, cannot truly "think outside the box." As a result, it is unlikely to independently discover groundbreaking solutions to complex global challenges such as climate change.

Balancing government intervention and economic growth while addressing China

In its strategic focus on China, the US must be careful not to overextend protectionist measures that could hinder growth. Overregulation risks stifling businesses, increasing compliance costs through added legal requirements, and reducing consumer demand as higher prices pass on the burden of regulations and taxes. Reshoring manufacturing is costly, and such efforts must be carefully balanced to avoid triggering a recession.

Controlling deficits and inflation remains a key priority. Persistent inflation could push interest rates higher, eroding productivity gains and discouraging investment in new ventures. Although the US approach to deficit reduction is still evolving, geopolitical pressures—such as rising military expenditures and the high costs of domestic industrial policy—could push interest rates higher and amplify economic challenges.

In this context, cost-cutting policies such as those associated with the US Department of Government Efficiency (DOGE) or insights from Mario Draghi's study on excessive EU regulations suggest a renewed focus on removing burdensome rules that constrain productivity and suppress GDP growth.

AI and technology: A unifying force for the Western world?

The US must address domestic political polarization by demonstrating the tangible benefits of AI and technological advancements. A strong model of economic growth driven by these innovations can help reassure the public by creating jobs, increasing wages across all sectors, and potentially reducing income inequalities. Additionally, transitioning to a green economy with sustainable jobs is crucial to meet the expectations of younger generations.

Beyond domestic considerations, AI and technology must also play a role in strengthening ties with key allies, including Europe, Japan, and potentially the Global South. It is not sufficient for the US to focus solely on producing superior products and exporting them worldwide. Relying on exports alone to overcome economic challenges may not be a sustainable strategy, as it could weaken allies who depend on US trade.

Technological advancements, particularly in AI, should not exclusively benefit the US but should contribute to the global effort to address rising greenhouse gas emissions. A collaborative approach that fosters mutual growth and sustainability is essential for long-term global prosperity.

Technology must also save the climate

AI and other new technologies could make all kinds of products more affordable—including green ones. This would support economic growth while also advancing sustainability goals. The green transition could move forward without slowing productivity and without relying on punishing carbon taxes to guide the economy in that direction.

Currently, AI and robotics are placing strain on power grids. To keep up, some major AI companies are investing in nuclear power. It is still unclear whether this will make nuclear energy more popular or simply take resources away from other green energy efforts. At the same time, AI firms are working on more efficient computer chips, but these will take years to spread widely.

The world can't afford to chase AI-driven growth while delaying the green transition and relying on fossil fuels. Sustainable development isn't optional. AI and new technologies need to help speed up, not slow down, the shift to a greener future.

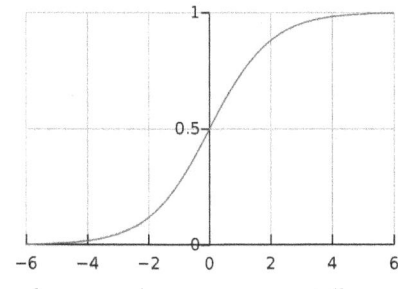

Many view technological innovation as the catalyst for environmental sustainability. Public fundamental research and private sector investments may soon facilitate the production of lightweight batteries, turnkey nuclear Generation IV power plants, and cheap solar panels. These advancements could supply energy at lower costs than fossil fuels, facilitating a swift transition to a carbon-neutral economy, potentially even without the need for subsidies or carbon-pricing mechanisms.

They forecast that clean energy and environmentally friendly products could rapidly become mainstream, following an S-curve pattern characterized by the swift adoption of innovations. This would entail a virtuous cycle of increasing production scale, decreasing prices, and further production enhancements, mirroring the historical adoption trends of gasoline-powered vehicles in the 1920s and smartphones in the 2010s. For instance, electric vehicles combined with cost-effective solar panels might outperform traditional gasoline-powered vehicles, achieving environmental goals through market forces rather than stringent regulatory measures.

There are counterarguments to this vision. An S-curve may not necessarily apply to the pricing of solar panels, wind turbines, or even SMR nuclear reactors, even if their production scales exponentially. This is due to their non-reducible transport and installation costs. Furthermore, resistance from certain segments of the population may emerge if they feel marginalized by these transitions. They could elect representatives opposing bans on gasoline-powered vehicles or the approval of permits for new nuclear facilities.

Compensating the Global South for green transition efforts

In addition to boosting their own economic growth, Western countries must also provide financial support to help developing nations transition to greener economies. The Global South, which faces significant climate-related challenges, has expressed concerns about the impacts of global warming—largely driven by emissions from industrialized nations over the past century.

A broader commitment from wealthier countries is essential. This includes offering compensation in the form of affordable access to green energy for countries in the Global South, which may not directly benefit from AI advancements yet are disproportionately affected by climate change.

Part 5

MONETARY ECONOMICS,

NOT POLITICS

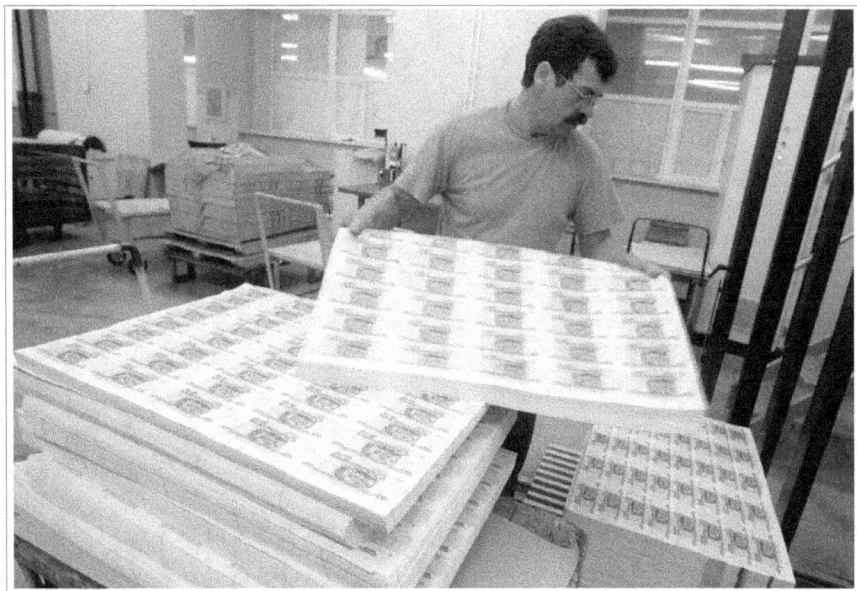

AI could help design cheaper, better green products with fewer workers—but it is unclear whether this would generate enough growth and many new jobs to contain global warming.

What is needed is a new economic framework supported by a fresh approach to money —much like how the Industrial Revolution was partly fueled by the introduction of paper banknotes alongside scarce precious-metal coins, enabling the purchase of new products. This kind of innovation puts money directly into consumers' hands, generating excitement and paving the way for an entirely new economy to emerge—potentially even a green one. Studying the history of money and understanding how monetary systems have evolved could inspire the next major economic transformation.

Monetary Changes Have Repeatedly Bypassed Politics

AI has the potential to boost productivity, but is it enough to steer the economy toward sustainability rather than merely fueling meaningless consumerism of leisure and gadgets? A greener economy could become a reality if the motivation to go green aligns with economic incentives. However, achieving this goal may require innovative approaches, such as rethinking product taxation and exploring new monetary strategies.

Monetary economics presents an opportunity for driving change. The idea of financing new ventures by modifying the existing monetary system is not novel. Historically, monetary systems have demonstrated remarkable adaptability, evolving from physical assets like silver and gold coins to today's digital representations of money in bank accounts. This evolution underscores the flexibility of monetary frameworks in responding to economic needs.

As in the books below, the next stage of monetary evolution could involve alternative currencies aimed at accelerating the velocity of money within a distinct economic market—separate from traditional and informal economies. This approach could unlock new opportunities for economic activity and contribute to tackling contemporary economic and environmental challenges.

FREE: A PARALLEL ECONOMY OUTSIDE THE REGULAR ACCOUNTING:
(Extract of the "History of Money for Understanding Economics")
Many believe that addressing global warming requires significant sacrifices, often advocating for strict regulations and penalties on fossil fuels—potentially at the expense of the poor.

For those with an interest in economics, the book The Green-Market System (excerpted from The History of Money for Understanding Economics) explores the concept of parallel currencies, both past and present, and proposes an amended monetary system. This system aims to stimulate a positive parallel economy that creates jobs and generates alternative income—without relying on punitive measures such as taxes and regulations.

FROM THE MUTATIONS OF THE MONETARY SYSTEM TO A PARALLEL CURRENCY:

The accessible book The History of Money for Understanding Economics delves into the evolution of the monetary system from its inception to the advent of digital currency, exploring its impact on historical events.

The book poses intriguing questions, such as whether the Roman Empire failed to industrialize (and survive) due to its inability to invent a new form of currency to finance new industries. In contrast, it highlights how Great Britain successfully industrialized in the 18th century by introducing banknotes made of inexpensive paper, which played a crucial role in financing its Industrial Revolution.

Looking ahead to the 21st century, the book speculates whether the modern world, currently grappling with persistent inequalities and the challenges of a green revolution, might require another transformation in its monetary system to move forward decisively, ultimately making politics a mere epiphenomenon of macroeconomics.

BIBLIOGRAPHY

The complete bibliography can be found in:
Lannoye, Vincent. The History of Money for Understanding Economics. 2015

6.

ORIGIN OF ILLUSTRATIONS